Praise for Jay DeCima's *Investing in Fixer-Uppers*

"Jay, I just want to say thank you! I read your book and was encouraged to finally step out and try my dream. It took a couple of months of looking and education, but I finally bought my first fixer project. I did it just like you said. I bought 2 houses together and after fix-up I have $340 positive cash flow. ... Thanks Jay for all the information."

—Marcus Shoemake

"My wife and I just read your book and really enjoyed it! We kind of stumbled into the 'fixer-up' business about a year ago by purchasing a foreclosure across the street. ... Your book couldn't have had a more appropriate title to catch our interest and inspire us to build more real estate wealth. Thanks for taking the time to write about all you've learned in the business."

—Dennis Keck

"I have just finished reading your excellent book, *Investing in Fixer-Uppers*. Many years ago I had the pleasure of reading the excellent Bill Nickerson books, and your publication certainly meets the standards that Nickerson had aspired to."

—Alan N. Scott

"I've just completed your book, *Investing in Fixer-Uppers*. I loved it. It was written in layman's terms so even a novice like myself, without any experience in real estate investing, could comprehend. Thank you for your time and for sharing your experience with us."

—Andre Guerra

"I recently purchased your book, *Investing in Fixer-Uppers*. It's the best real estate book I've ever read. It is the perfect guide for a beginning investor."

—Richard Miller

"I recently purchased and read your book. It's, without a doubt, a wonderful source of inspiration, as well as information that I'm planning to put to work soon."

—Cesar Rodriguez

"I just finished reading your book, *Investing in Fixer-Uppers*. This is the best book I've read on becoming a real estate investor. It's really a real estate investor start-up handbook. I congratulate you!"

—Luis L. Lozada

"Wow! Your book is the best by far—leaps and bounds over other real estate books I've read. I own a rental house, free and clear. Now cash flow keeps me green and growing, I understand landlording and how to acquire a fixer-up property, and so much more. Wow, what a book!"

—Curtis Harris

"I have been investing in real estate in the Chicagoland area going on my second year now. I have been reading books, going to seminars, taking courses, etc. for about seven years. ... This is the best real estate investing guide I have ever read. Over seven years I have probably read 40 to 50 books about real estate investment, some old, some new, some terrible. I urge anyone interested in investing in real estate to buy this book! ... Great job!"

—Joe Mueller

"I just finished reading your book, *Investing in Fixer-Uppers*, and I enjoyed it immensely. I have been doing a lot of 'brain compounding' lately, reading and learning as much as I can about real estate. Some of the books I've read were very vague in terms of subject matter or filled with a lot of hype. Your book, on the other hand, was very informative and well written. I could understand the concept of your investment strategies and your overall approach on the fixer-upper. I will definitely use your book as a resource when I take action and buy my first fixer house. Thanks again for a great book!"

—Brian Maston

"As a young, future real estate investor still crafting a business plan, I am constantly seeking diverse sources of quality ideas. I must say that among the literally dozens of property investment texts I have taken on since starting my research at age 20, this one of yours has to be among a handful of those most worthy of the time spent. I found your chapters on fix-up strategy, designing money partnerships, and buying back your own financing notes at a discount particularly instructive and inspiring."

—Matthew A. Adams, CORE Capitalist Partners

"I would like to thank you for taking the time to write your book, *Investing in Fixer-Uppers*. I'm a 27-year-old single male who was just interested in buying and selling single-family homes. After reading your book, you really inspired me to do more than just that."

—Robert Dodds

Start Small, Profit Big in Real Estate

Also from McGraw-Hill

Jay P. DeCima, *Investing in Fixer-Uppers: A Complete Guide to Buying Low, Fixing Smart, Adding Value, and Selling (or Renting) High*

Start Small, Profit Big in Real Estate

Fixer Jay's 2-Year Plan for Building Wealth—Starting from Scratch!

Jay P. DeCima

McGraw-Hill

New York Chicago San Francisco Lisbon London
Madrid Mexico City Milan New Delhi San Juan
Seoul Singapore Sydney Toronto

The **McGraw·Hill** Companies

4 5 6 7 8 9 0 DOC/DOC 0 9 8 7 6

ISBN 0-07-144380-0

Editorial and production services provided by CWL Publishing Enterprises, Inc., Madison, WI, www.cwlpub.com.

This publication is designed to provide accurate and authoritative information in regard to the subject matter covered. It is sold with the understanding that neither the author nor the publisher is engaged in rendering legal, accounting, or other professional service. If legal advice or other expert assistance is required, the services of a competent professional person should be sought.
> —*From a Declaration of Principles jointly adopted by a Committee of the American Bar Association and a Committee of Publishers*

McGraw-Hill books are available at special quantity discounts to use as premiums and sales promotions, or for use in corporate training programs. For more information, please write to the Director of Special Sales, McGraw-Hill, 2 Penn Plaza, New York, NY 10128. Or contact your local bookstore.

Library of Congress Cataloging-in-Publication Data

DeCima, Jay P.
   Start small, profit big in real estate : Fixer Jay's 2-year plan for building wealth—starting from scratch! / by Jay P. DeCima.
     p. cm.
  Includes bibliographical references and index.
  ISBN 0-07-144380-0 (pbk. : alk. paper)
   1. Real estate investment—United States. 2. Housing rehabilitation—United States. 3. Rental housing—United States—Maintenance and
  repair.
  I. Title.
  HD255.D44 2005
  332.63'24—dc22

                        2004023702

Contents

Contents

Contents

Contents

Contents

Contents

Introduction

In 1969, my real estate license was mailed to the broker at Forestland Realty, located in the small town of Jackson, in the heart of California's gold country. It was my first job as a real estate salesman. By the year's end I had earned $7,200 in commissions. Not too bad for a start, I figured, but still far short of my million-dollar dreams.

Mr. Roper, my real estate instructor, taught me enough so that I could pass the examination on the very first go-around. At the time, I remember thinking he was the smartest instructor in the world. But as things turned out, passing the real estate examination is not the reason I'm still thankful to Mr. Roper today. Instead, it was a casual remark he made to the entire class of 76 students. Here's what Mr. Roper said: "Commissions will not make any of you rich! Rich folks," he said, "are the ones who get their names typed on deeds. They are the property owners."

He then told us a simple formula for becoming wealthy. He said we should all invest 10 percent of all our commissions in income properties that would earn us money even while we were sleeping. At the time I didn't pay much attention to Mr. Roper's advice. To me, it seemed like commissions would make me a whole lot richer than rents—and more quickly too. It took me a few more years before I would finally test Mr. Roper's advice. I purchased four fixer-upper houses and began my journey toward living off the rents I collected.

Lots of water has passed under the bridge since I bought those first four houses. Along the way I discovered that run-down property had lots more cash flow than properties in better shape. They also were three or four times more profitable than pretty properties. I also found out that you don't need to be a Harvard graduate to make a lot of money fixing up houses. Once you learn what to do, you can keep repeating it until you reach whatever income level you choose. Before I sold off a few houses several years back, my rents had reached nearly $100,000 a month. Naturally, I've got expenses like everyone else; but I will tell you right now, I'm still head and shoulders above any commissions I ever dreamed of making.

During the past 20 years or so, I've been teaching seminars about making big money with houses by investing in fixer-upper properties. You can call them ugly if you like, 'cause that's what I call 'em too! One of the questions I'm most frequently asked is, "Isn't there a lot of extra work involved in fixing up run-down houses?" Of course there's work, but it's not nearly as difficult as most folks think. In my best-selling book, *Investing in Fixer-Uppers*, I explain why I'm the highest-paid plumber in my town. If that weren't true, there's no way in the world I'd do it, believe me. Money makes plumbing a lot easier. The truth is you don't even need to be a plumber, painter, or electrician. The reason is that 85 percent of fix-up is just plain, ordinary cleanup.

Folks also ask, "How hard is it to earn $100,000 every month in rents?" When you first get started, it will seem impossible. However, once you begin to learn the ropes, it becomes much easier. First, you'll make $1,000, and before long you'll reach $5,000. The thing I like most about my way of investing is that you can quit at 10 houses or keep going on past 200 like I did. That's up to you! If you read my book and only acquire three or four solid income-producing properties, you'll be a lot better off than you are right now.

Real estate opportunities have never been better for do-it-yourself wealth builders as we begin a brand new century. Naturally, I'm referring to the kind of properties I write about—investment houses and small rental properties—the kind of real estate that earns me a very handsome living, same as it does for many of my readers.

A Stable and Predictable Future If You Stay Focused

Two of the major benefits in this business are that it continues to be very stable and it's almost always predictable. Unlike the blacksmiths, railroad caboose conductors, and junk bond sellers, you can expect to enjoy a long-term prosperous career and a very rosy future if you invest in affordable income properties as I recommend.

A few words of caution are appropriate here because of the many letters and telephone calls I receive asking my opinion about various other types of investment opportunities. Do not get sidetracked. You must constantly be on guard against the TV hucksters and others who expound softer, easier, and faster programs, which they claim can quickly make you wealthy. Years ago, I discovered this particular weakness in my own mentality. Sometimes, when I listened to those too-good-to-be-true types of pitches, I would catch myself thinking (perhaps I was dreaming) that just maybe they might work for me. Fortunately for me, my practical side would always rule the day. I've since concluded that we folks who are motivated to achieve a little extra in the shortest possible time are just naturally suckers for all those slick-sounding promotions. My advice is to keep buying houses, and eventually you'll outgrow the urge to look elsewhere. Temptation to stray off course is something we must all resist.

A Wealth-Building Plan for the Whole Family

People who hear me lecture or read my newsletters probably already know about the multiple wealth-building benefits available to families who invest together—family investment teams, I call them. I don't know of any better plan for generating the extra money needed for the kids' college education than operating a well-planned family real estate partnership. With my value-adding strategy (fixing houses), there's hardly any risk involved. Parents can selectively acquire income properties while the kids learn to repair things, handle responsibilities, and manage the houses in order to earn their college money (the rental income). Besides the money, this is a one-of-a-kind on-the-job training experience where the kids can develop some practical business skills. Best of all you can do it from your own home. I owned and managed 45 rentals before I outgrew my kitchen table. It's a winning proposition for all involved.

My good friend Dave earns $3,400 extra every month from his rental houses. Rental houses bought his boys new trucks and paid for their schooling. When my friend sells the houses, he plans to carry back secured notes, which will more than triple his retirement income. Not bad for nine rental houses, working part time.

Everyone can do this stuff, but as I said earlier, you need to learn the ropes. My advice is simple: Learn the business from people who do this stuff. Obviously, I can teach you, but certainly I'm not the only one. Fixing run-down houses is a high-profit business that doesn't depend on appreciation and bank loans. It works in good times and in bad times, and, last but equally important, it's very low-risk investing. For example, let's assume the kids take to real estate like ducks take to water. It's very likely that they'll be successful and do quite well. They might even make the family filthy rich in the process. On the flip side, suppose the family invests in property, and the kids turn out to be lazy bums and derelicts. Chances are good you'll still come out ahead on the deal, even though you might end up doing all the work yourself. Generally, the most you would likely lose is the potential profits you might have earned had things worked out. Still, from what I have observed to date, most families who invest together and share the wealth with each other always seem to come out much stronger than those who pass up this golden opportunity.

Profits in a Short Period of Time and Personal Freedom

Operating income properties from your kitchen table can become a very profitable venture in a relatively short period of time. However, you must learn to use good business strategies, starting with your very first deal. Since we're on the subject of starting, let me toss out an important tip here. One of the biggest mistakes made by inexperienced investors is to treat the house business like a hobby. If you do that, your earnings will end up just like those from most hobbies. Don't forget, one small rental house is a business the same as 100 rental houses are. The only difference is the size. Probably the most difficult task for house investors is handling the tenants. Obviously, that's one area where good business skills are critical.

People often ask me, "What do you enjoy most about being your own boss? Is it making more money, or is it the freedom to spend your time doing the things you really want to do?" The answer is both. The way I see it, life would be very dull indeed if I had to spend all my waking hours stacking my real estate earnings in a room and guarding them. What would be the purpose in that? On the other hand, without cash flow or profits, I certainly wouldn't be able to do all the things I like to do with my personal freedom.

I shall always be grateful to Mr. Roper for convincing me that investing in income-producing real estate is truly the path that leads to financial independence. I have since discovered it's also the same path that leads to genuine personal freedom. Real estate investing has given me the opportunity to control my personal life and earn enough money to live very comfortably.

An Expert's View of the Future

In conclusion, two important questions need answering. First, what does the future look like for this business? And, second, what are the odds of becoming a successful (wealthy) housing entrepreneur?

The rental housing business needs all the help it can get. Growing numbers of young people don't earn enough money to buy a home for their families. That translates to more and more renters who will need rental houses. Recent tax laws have greatly slowed down apartment construction by eliminating the once overly generous tax shelters the big developers sought. Affordable rental housing shortages now exist everywhere. The U.S. Department of Housing and Urban Development (HUD) stopped building new properties years ago, and with the federal budget shortages caused by military spending and social programs, they're not likely to start again. With a record number of foreclosed properties, including REOs (Real Estate Owned), available, the rules are changing. Changing rules almost always deal a deathblow to the inflexible. However, the same changes offer new hope and opportunity to those who are willing to meet new challenges.

Introduction

The fact is that more houses are becoming fix-up candidates than are being fixed. HUD estimates that 500,000 units of residential housing are falling below minimum habitability standards annually. That number is somewhat baffling given the amount of money HUD spends annually to provide safe, adequate housing for low-income families. However, it's good news for us house fixers. Fixing up run-down houses is a great opportunity with a very bright future indeed.

What all this means is that there's a huge demand with more customers than ever before. The shortage of affordable rental housing plus more and more renters are almost an ironclad guarantee that housing entrepreneurs can expect a very prosperous future for many years to come. Fixing houses is the best new career I know of, and there's hardly any serious competition to slow you down when you do it my way.

PART 1

Planning to Make Money

1

Achieving Financial Independence

In this chapter you will learn about:

- Selecting the right property and finding motivated sellers
- Doubling your property value in 24 months
- Earning $100,000 annually in the early years
- Earning extra cash starting out

Have you ever wondered what it would be like if you didn't have a regular job? I don't mean that you wouldn't work anymore. What I'm talking about here is working for yourself instead. Working for yourself is different. To start with, the more effort you put out, the more you'll benefit yourself. Think about this for a moment. Usually it doesn't work that way. When you are an employee, more often than not your extra efforts only benefit the company. That's one important difference when it comes to achieving your personal financial goals.

Jay Earns 17 Times More Than a Real Estate Agent

For example, when I fix up rental houses for monthly cash or to sell for a profit, all the money I earn from my efforts is mine to keep. When you work for someone else, it's not the least bit uncommon to make thousands of dollars for the company, yet profit very little extra for yourself. I often explain this earning discrepancy to real estate agents who ask me if I think owning properties is more profitable than selling them.

Let's say I purchase a $100,000 income property for $80,000. When I buy the property through my agent, he will earn 6 percent commission or $4,800. Generally he gets to keep only $2,400 for himself, and that's it. My earnings are a whole lot different. First, there's my $20,000 of nontaxable up-front profit or discount for having the know-how to buy a property under market value. Next, I'll probably fix up the property, raise the rents, and enjoy monthly cash flow. Finally, I may choose to do a three-year lease/option agreement, selling the property for $120,000 by offering very attractive terms. It doesn't take a mathematical genius to see that, by working for myself, I have substantial financial advantages. I have the flexibility of earning money in several different ways. In the example above, my agent nets $2,400, while I will earn a profit of $40,000 on the same property. That's almost 17 times more profit. Needless to say, it's also one of the secrets of becoming financially independent in the shortest possible time.

Besides the money, being your own boss gives you many choices. My first choice I often call the "ultimate freedom." There's no more dreading Monday mornings or driving the crowded freeways before it's even daylight. Hassles with the boss about "passed over" promotions, piddly cost-of-living raises, and boring job assignments are all memories of the past.

Believe me, no one ever invented a better way to earn a living and have so much personal freedom doing it.

Many years ago, I quit the telephone company job I'd spent 23 years at. At first I was afraid I might starve to death, but I didn't. I was constantly worried about losing my company-paid health insurance, but soon I was earning enough money to pay for my own. I think the fear of losing a steady paycheck (every two weeks) bothered me most. Those fears all disappeared when I sold my first fixed-up rental property for a bigger profit than two years' worth of telephone company paychecks added together. Looking back now, I can honestly tell you that the fear of change will be your biggest obstacle. It's the uncertainty of what will happen next. Obviously, no one gets any guarantees. However, I can tell you from experience that most fears are easy to overcome with knowledge. As you develop your personal skills, confidence gradually pushes fear behind you. Of course, that's hindsight; no one told me that when I first started out.

Selecting the Right Property

Many folks fully understand that there's a lot of money to be made in real estate, but, beyond that, they understand little else, such as what kind of real estate is best. Simply owning real estate is not enough—many people buy real estate and go broke. When you first begin looking, most real estate available for sale will not be the right kind for making the accelerated profits that I'm discussing. You must first convert your thinking about real estate buying into benefits and circumstances. This takes a bit of getting used to, but once you get the hang of it, finding the right real estate will become a much more focused process for you. You'll automatically stop wasting valuable time with real estate that won't turn a profit. Successful real estate investors know how to find properties with high-profit potential and leave the losers behind.

When you're making your first property purchase, keep in mind that maximum benefits come from sellers who want *you* to own their property more than *they* want to. I could shorten that sentence to say that sellers must be motivated, but I want this point to be crystal clear. You can't make big money from sellers who don't have any serious reason to sell. A good rule to remember is that you must never want a property more than the sellers want to sell it. If this happens, he or she controls the transaction, and you'll likely end up losing out. The multiple benefits (we discuss in lots more detail) will come from sellers who have problems and are seeking relief.

Residential income properties offer the best and safest choice for most start-out investors. It's been my investment of choice for many years, even though I have tons of experience with other kinds of real estate investments. Residential properties, whether you plan to rent them out or fix them up for resale, will take the least amount of knowledge; therefore, it makes good sense to begin there. In terms of risk (as in safe investment), it's difficult to lose much money if you don't grossly overpay to begin with.

I'm about to let you in on a plan for investing that won't cost you a ton of money to get started. You can do it part time and quite easily double your current income or keep on going until your real estate becomes a full-time job as it did for me. If you follow my strategies, you'll be learning the business through hands-on experience, and your financial risk will be minimal if you buy properties as I suggest. You could lose a few hours of personal labor if things don't work out. But I'm sure you'll agree with me that using your own labor while you're learning the ropes is a cheap price to pay for an unlimited profit potential. Investing in the kind of real estate I recommend has many unique advantages, but topping the list is the quick payback. My goal is to double the property value in a span of just 24 months. With run-down rental units, I intend to increase rents by 50 percent during the same time frame. Adding value is the magic, and there's no other kind of real estate investing I know of that brings home the profits any quicker. Fixing up run-down properties (adding value) allows you to invest anytime, anywhere, because it does not rely on appreciation or the economy to earn profits. The profits simply depend on your skills.

How to Double the Value in 24 Months

Let me explain why my kind of investing works so well. Both renters and buyers want clean, attractive houses to own and live in. Most buyers are not the least bit interested in hearing about the property's potential. The fact is, most people cannot begin to visualize the drastic changes that take place when a filthy "dirt-bag" property is fixed up, cleaned, and painted. Simply cleaning and hauling away the junk can make a dramatic difference with ugly run-down properties. It's just human nature to associate neat and clean with higher value.

Filthy houses in pigsty condition are depressing to look at. So are skuzzy occupants hanging out the windows. These conditions are the reasons why most investors will drive on by, stop their house hunting, and go have pizza instead. However, to the trained eye of a knowledgeable investor, these houses can very well be hidden gold mines with valuable treasures beneath layers of filth and neglect. My investment strategy is not much different from that of a gold miner. My gold comes from turning ugly-duckling houses into beautiful-looking swans. The magic is my ability to create good looks where ugliness once existed. This quick switch from ugly to attractive is the fastest method I know to create large equities and predictable income all in one swoop. Ugly real estate attracts very few serious buyers. Most simply lack the imagination and the skills needed to turn these properties into high-profit houses. If you are willing to educate yourself and look beyond the dirt and grime, you'll discover, as I have, that ugliness is only skin-deep and that a little effort can make a huge value change in very little time.

Keep in mind that investment houses are not all created equal nor do they provide equal benefits. If you were to purchase average rental houses in average neighborhoods, not surprisingly, you'll likely have average cash flow. The problem is it's negative. Negative cash flow is for wimps, not tycoons. That strategy will get you nowhere. If you would like a business that has great cash returns, look for run-down "El Dumpo" houses in acceptable neighborhoods (that means no wars going on) that will respond well to "inexpensive fine-tuning" (fix-up) using cheap labor. Cheap labor means you'll probably be doing the job yourself. This strategy is a quick cash flow generator. Since El Dumpo houses don't look too good or smell very nice, you can buy them cheaply and with very liberal terms. Once you learn a few negotiating skills, you'll be able to acquire these kind of houses almost anywhere. All it takes is to get started and practice.

How Long Will It Take, and How Much Can I Make?

How long will it take to be successful, and how much money can you make? I've combined these two questions because everyone thinks they should go together. Two years after you acquire your first property, you should have a dependable income, assuming that you're following my strategies. How much, of course, depends on you and your property selection. Obviously, there is no "one size fits all" answer to getting rich, and there's no clear dollar amount that will signal when you've arrived.

To me rich comes in two different flavors: "stay-at-home rich" and "super rich." Stay-at-home rich means you don't need an outside job. You are your own boss; you have enough money from your investments to support your lifestyle. Super rich means that you are totally funded for the remainder of your life on the planet. You can do and pay for almost anything you choose. Obviously one could quarrel over dollar amounts, but for our purpose here, I think you can see the distinction.

Stay-at-home rich is attainable by almost everyone reading this book. Therefore, we'll make that our goal. Before I leave this subject, let me remind you that both flavors of rich will take education, persistence, and hard work on your part. The only difference is that one takes much more of the same, but that's it.

In my early years, it simply never occurred to me that buying houses was a business opportunity. I thought I was just a regular, everyday, garden-variety real estate investor and that was that. Looking back today, I stand corrected. I was just beginning a journey that would make me a wealthy businessman.

Investing in Real Estate Is Like Kissing Frogs

Taking advantage of new opportunities means knowing what to do and how to do it. You must be willing to roll up your sleeves and go for it. You alone are the person who must make it happen. Making things happen is a lot like kissing frogs. Chances are you'll need to kiss a lot of frogs before you finally meet a prince. You cannot stay inside the comforts of your house and wait for the frogs to hop in and kiss you. You've got to spend many hours of your time with the frogs. Remember, most frogs are hiding deep in the muddy marshes. Kissing frogs is a contact sport. You cannot ask your friends, your real estate broker, or your secretary to do it for you. They haven't got the stomach for it. You can't keep changing kissing styles either, because one seems easier than the other; and you can't spend all your time in kissing school. That's not the way you'll find a prince. Also, don't be kissing the same frog 40 times. It shouldn't take that much smooching to tell a frog from a prince. Kissing frogs is like investing in real estate. The more time and effort you put in, the more experience you gain. After a while, you'll be able to tell if you have a prince on the very first kiss. The point I'm making here is simple. Forget about shortcuts—there are none. Don't worry about how fast the folks on TV are getting rich. Remember, that's showbiz, and we're investors!

A Business with Real Estate Assets

A housing entrepreneur, which is what I consider myself, is a businessperson with real estate assets. It's somewhat different from what most folks think of when they consider going into business for themselves. They normally think more about owning a hamburger stand, buying a carpet cleaning franchise with a special-built steam cleaner truck, acquiring an ice cream and Popsicle route, or perhaps setting up a silkscreen T-shirt factory. Typically, these kinds of businesses don't have much long-term appreciating value, and they seldom provide much more than steady employment for their owners. In several cases I'm familiar with, the operators feel quite fortunate to earn what I'd call average wages. Often their actual take-home pay would be higher if they worked for someone else, plus they wouldn't have their own money tied up in the business. Let me say it this way—many folks who are dedicated to a wide variety of small businesses work very hard. They put in twice as many hours for a lot less pay than they could expect to take home as regular employees. This situation can be a big temptation for people like me and others who often harbor a blind obsession to be their own boss.

A student of mine bought a fancy air machine that blows up balloons with your picture on them. It looks like a portable "outhouse" on wheels. He tows it around to shopping malls and county fairs. It has a built-in camera, a hot-air blower, and a special foldout work counter. The glossy full-color business opportunity brochure says it will pay for itself in about five years if the owner works on weekends. At the rate my friend is selling balloons, he figures it'll take about 18 years. Smart people often do the strangest things for money. I'm sure the promoter blows a lot more hot air than my friend's air machine does.

It's generally best to start out with a small rental house or a group of several units. Generally $5,000 or $10,000 is more than enough cash to start. Many investors start out with less when they don't have it. My entrepreneurial friend is paying twice that much on his hot-air contract. All together, it will cost him $38,000 with the interest added on. All he'll ever own, from what I can see, is hot air, a worn-out blower, and a bag of leftover balloons.

It's my personal view that working for yourself is the ultimate freedom, but there's no thrill in being your own boss if you can't make a decent living to support yourself and your family. This brings us to what I consider the safest and most profitable business opportunity today—the business of income-producing real estate.

The combination of a cash flow business that owns appreciating real estate assets is truly the best of all worlds. In my case, the houses are my widgets. I'm in the business of renting or selling residential space to my customers. My business assets are houses. Instead of losing value as they become more used, they are instead becoming increasingly more valuable. Even if my stream of rental customers slows down from time to time, will I go broke? Not very likely, because my real estate assets have been continually growing in value. That value is easily converted to cash if I need grocery money, either by borrowing on my equity or by selling a house or two.

Ways to Earn Extra Cash When You Start

New investors can find a variety of ways to earn extra cash in the investment housing business, depending on where they are financially when they start. One method I used successfully, when I was first starting out, was to manage properties for other investors. I did fix-up work and received pay from the owners. Sometimes I was allowed to keep the cash flow, which kept increasing as I improved the properties. In some cases, I negotiated an option to purchase half the equity when I fixed up the property. I also received finder's fees for locating good deals. Finder's fees, compensation for fix-up work, and being allowed to keep a portion of the rental income do not require having a real estate license. You simply don't need a bundle of money to get started, if you begin to think creatively. Make a real effort to use whatever personal skills you have. Why not turn them into down payments?

Achieve Any Financial Goal You Set

When I purchased my first four rental houses on Pine Street, earning $100,000 annually as a real estate investor was far beyond my comprehension. Nevertheless, in less than two years I sold the property for almost double what I originally paid. My goals were much smaller back then, even though I heard others say it was possible. Not only was it possible for me, but it's also become a reality for many other investors who have learned from my teachings along the way. If I ever had any notions about having some special talent that no one else could duplicate, that idea has long been shattered. The fact is that a growing number of my students have actually surpassed me in terms of wealth. Naturally, I must confess, students passing up their teacher is not too good for one's ego, although it reflects very well on me.

Regardless of who makes the most money, the thing that's important to remember is that you can achieve almost any financial goal you set for yourself. When you prepare yourself and learn what to do, $100,000 annually is nowhere near the high-water mark in this business. In fact, that's just about the average for an ordinary mom-and-pop team after several years of learning (education) and doing this stuff the right way. I say doing stuff right because that's really the key to your success. Many first-time students have said to me, "Jay, I really like all your ideas and techniques, but here's how folks do things in my town." Friends, that's not the proper mode for your brain to be in if you expect to learn new skills. Being stuck in the wrong mode is the way to keep buying negative cash flow houses, tax shelters that don't shelter anything, and properties that are not likely to turn a profit.

Here's the bottom line. If you're searching for a better mousetrap, do-it-yourself real estate investing might just answer all your prayers. Obviously, learning new methods to earn money will require a big effort on your part. But if you start now, you'll be pleasantly surprised at how fast you can accomplish the task. Whether your goal is to simply earn additional income or fully commit yourself to full-time investing, like I did, the choice is yours. However, the knowledge you'll need is exactly the same. I might just add that opportunities to earn big money investing in real estate have never been better. Do-it-yourself investing, the way I teach it, is quite predictable with very minimal risk. Also, it won't cost you a ton of money to get started. Regular, everyday folks can still achieve financial independence. Plus, consider how much less complicated your life might be if your office was also your kitchen table. No freeways, no babysitters, and no strict time schedules to follow. The kitchen table is still my favorite desk after doing this stuff for more than 40 years, but I did add that extra leaf when I needed more space for counting rent money.

2

Early Planning Pays

In this chapter you will learn about:

- Setting goals
- Selecting an investment vehicle
- Properties to avoid
- How to write off the risk factor

Everyone dances to different music. Ask yourself these questions: What do I really want? What does my family want? When families are involved, it's very important that everyone be part of the early planning. Nothing sets the stage for disaster quicker than having one member of a family dedicated to full-time real estate investing, while the other members are not the least bit interested. It's much better to continue investing on a part-time basis until all family members are equally enthusiastic and willing to support career changing. Believe me, it takes 100-percent cooperation to make it. Don't start with anything less.

Full-time investing is not meant for everyone. However, I think the door is wide open for people who set their minds to doing it. It takes guts, determination, and knowledge, but the rewards are worth it. I can still remember the day I quit my telephone company job. Friends congratulated me. Secretly, many thought I was nuts. Some said my timing was good, while others said it was lousy. Others just shook their heads and smiled. I heard them mumble something about "midlife crisis." I'm first to admit that during those early moments I felt somewhat insecure. But the feeling didn't last. When my telephone company friends heard about the $200,000 profit I made after I sold 11 small houses, they said, "Jay's the luckiest guy we know. He got into real estate at just the perfect time. He was sure lucky to find that property when he did. He must have had some hidden money to get started." My telephone company friends had come full circle. On the day I quit, they thought I was nuts. Now they'd decided I was lucky too.

Many people I know have hardly anything to lose, yet they act as though they are protecting great wealth. Any risk at all seems to bother them. It's difficult for me to understand their thinking. I have friends who buy tons of insurance to protect everything they own, yet their true net worth is peanuts. If they were sued in court, I think they'd be shocked to find out their insurance premiums add up to more dollars than the value of possessions they insure.

My message is simply this: Think about what you have today. What will you be giving up? Ask yourself this question: Would I be better off doing something different? If you don't have much now and your future seems uncertain, you may have very little to lose. But don't throw caution to the wind or dream up wild ideas. Think it out thoroughly. Then act.

Choose Your Teachers Carefully

Why is it that very few people ever achieve their financial dreams? What do the few successful ones do differently from the majority who fail? Could it be they plan to fail? I don't think so. It's more likely they fail to plan. Many folks waste much of their most valuable resource, their own time, trying to figure out ways to make money quickly and easily without any effort. These people are only fooling themselves. Nothing worthwhile is accomplished without a plan and without some hard work.

For several years after I began investing in run-down rental houses, it seemed like the TV channels were crammed with late-night cable programs featuring a variety of get-rich gurus. At the time I was working 16 hours a day, every day—writing offers, buying properties, and fixing run-down houses. One of the reasons I happened to watch so many get-rich real estate programs on TV was because they came on just about the same time I'd be wrapping up for the day. I'd grab a quick bite to eat and watch TV while I read through the classified ads. These gurus promised that if I followed their simple advice and did exactly as instructed, I could easily become a millionaire within a year or so. I remember how depressed I would get when I compared my own results with the late-night testimonials from the scores of get-rich followers. Many claimed they were making thousands of dollars on every deal.

I remember a 23-year-old carpet layer from Los Angeles who said he made $56,000 during one weekend. A lady from Tulsa, Oklahoma, bought two brick duplexes for nothing down. She got $12,000 at the closing. Then she claimed she would earn $450 per month from now until the cows come home. One of the most discouraging TV programs for me was the night they had a blind guest. He was in a wheelchair, and they rolled him out on the stage. He had his hands full of closing papers, showing how he bought a warehouse on Tuesday for $400,000, and then on Friday, just three days later, he sold the property for $560,000, using back-to-back escrow closings. He claimed profits like this ($160,000) are easy if you know the right forms to use. $160,000 in three days, wow! I had to be doing something wrong. I wasn't even close to these guys. I thought, even a blind man who couldn't see the houses or drive to the property was beating the socks off me. Sleep came much faster than the answer. Working 16 hours a day doesn't leave much time for wondering about what they do on TV shows. Still, I was determined. I just kept fixing up my houses and tried to ignore the guys on TV.

Since then I've become much wiser. Two important facts have become increasingly clear to me. First, and most important, it's true that regular, ordinary folks can make a great deal of money investing in real estate. You don't need a lot of money to start, and you don't need any extra special talents to begin with. However, you can't expect to end up wealthy and financially independent unless you are willing to pay the price of admission. Simply stated, you need a reasonable and workable plan. Then you must work that plan. Often hard work can be greatly reduced by smart work, but generally this doesn't happen until you are well into your plan and have reached a certain level of experience. Seldom can one get the experience without the hard work initially. It just so happens this is one of the rules for success. The second fact I've learned is also very important. What you see and what you hear ain't necessarily the way it really is. You can take my word on that.

Never Try to Milk a Steer

Making a million dollars in real estate is a lot harder than most people say it is. That's the bad news, but there is some good news too. Making the second million is a good deal easier than most folks think it is. Strange how it works that way—and I think I can tell you the reason why. You see, most instructors who teach people how easy it is haven't done it themselves, so they really don't know how. Most investors who have made a million starting from scratch get very protective about their hard-earned wealth and likely won't tell you anything. Naturally, there are a few exceptions, but if you follow the money trail, the reasons often become quite clear. Most investors or wannabes are much better off staying away from strategies that sound slick. Slick is another word for slippery, which means hard to hang onto. Over the past 10 years or so, I can recall the names of a least a dozen so-called real estate gurus who expounded on a wide assortment of get-rich techniques. Most of these "experts" are either bankrupt or working at a gas station today. One cable TV personality has moved onto a new field, selling car wax and used videotapes. The moral to this story is that you should always check out your mentors. You can get milk only from a dairy cow.

Every once in a while even dummies make money in real estate. But take my advice, and don't give up your day job thinking it happens often, because it doesn't. A far more realistic approach is to learn exactly how and why real estate profits are made to begin with. If you do this, you'll be in a position to make money in good times and bad times alike. Also, you won't need to depend on appreciation to make your profit. Appreciation earnings should be a bonus for investing wisely.

Know Your Destination and Vehicle

When you begin your journey to financial independence, the first thing you must do is determine where you want to go—establish your target, goal, or destination. Next, you must decide how you will get there, how you plan to accomplish these. What are the risks, rewards, and sacrifices? Are they worth the end results? Don't complicate your plan. No one likes to follow a plan that's overloaded with restrictions and contingencies. Keep it simple. Let me give you an example of a plan I know best. It's my own personal plan for financial independence, investing in do-it-yourself real estate.

When I started, I had certain limitations. The first one is somewhat common and almost everyone has it—very little cash to invest. Second, I had very little knowledge about investing. Third, and almost as important as the others, was that I could only spare so much time to do my real estate investing. I had my regular day job, too. Real estate investing would have to be done in addition to my regular job. As it turned out, I did both jobs for a couple of years before I was able to quit the telephone company job and support myself with real estate profits. Looking back now, I still wonder where I found the time to do it all. It was hard work, but it was certainly worth all the effort I gave it.

Let's review. The first part of my plan is knowing where you want to go—the destination. In my case, I wanted to own enough income-producing real estate to support the lifestyle I planned for myself, which meant I'd need to own rental properties that would provide enough cash flow every month to pay for that lifestyle. I remember at first that $1,000 every month was OK. Then $2,000 seemed more appropriate. When I achieved the $2,000, I adjusted my goal to $3,000, then $5,000 and so forth. Remember, when you're working your plan, adjustments and fine-tuning are perfectly all right. Also, don't forget what I told you about working smart.

The second part of my plan involves knowing how to get to your destination—the vehicle. This part is also very important. You must choose a method for achieving your goals (fix-up properties) that suits your personal capabilities, both financially and physically. You must know yourself and your limitations before you begin. I'm always baffled by folks who attempt to do things beyond their capabilities. Just recently I counseled an older gentleman about a trust deed investment he had purchased. He received the first two payments, and then they stopped. Everything about the deal was bad. The property was in another state. The building wasn't rented. An appraisal had been done by a real estate agent who was also a principal. The deed was a third instead of a second as he told me. (First, second, and third is the priority of the deed based on the date it was recorded in the county records.) And, worst of all, I couldn't find a smidgen of equity. This guy didn't have the foggiest idea about how to get his $21,000 investment back. My guess is he won't. Continually evaluate what you can do and what you cannot do. This is not the place to dream. In my own case, I had very little money saved. Money to start, as it turns out, is much less important than starting and continuing. Persistence will be the most important ingredient of your plan.

A Simple Plan—Reasonable and Profitable

I decided to buy older houses and small apartments that needed fixing up. My reasoning was that I could do much of the work myself, plus I could buy the properties for much less cash down because there are fewer serious buyers for unsightly, distressed properties. I also thought, and it proved to be true, that once fixed and cleaned up with bright new paint, older rental houses would command about the same rents as equivalent-sized newer houses. The same thing is true with older run-down apartments, although I've always favored houses because tenants will always rent houses quicker than they will apartments.

The best thing you can do to prepare for success is to develop a total investment plan from start to finish. I recommend specializing to begin with. Say you plan to buy four rental fix-up properties each year for five years. Each one must produce $100 monthly. That's a reasonable plan. Don't ask me which strategy is best—fix and sell or fix and rent. They're both best. I think it has to do with the individual. Also, if you need the money from your first fix-up job in order to continue, selling may be your only option.

Let me share a little secret. Finding good properties (good deals) is one of my most difficult tasks. When I find one that I can fix up and increase rents to produce steady monthly income, it hurts me to sell it. You'll be pleasantly surprised when you find out how quickly positive monthly income adds to your wealth. I'm a firm believer in keeping the goose that lays big golden eggs. The key, I believe, is to start fixing and try them both yourself. Again, I emphasize it's always best to learn as you are doing. Many people start with fixer-uppers. Then over time they gradually switch to other investment specialties. That's a perfectly acceptable and reasonable strategy. Others like me develop a special knack for fixing houses and generating a very handsome cash flow from the added value, so we just keep doing it.

It is not my purpose here to explain why my plan has worked out so well financially, other than to say big money is made in real estate when you can consistently get the highest return on your investment. Let me ask you a question. Which do you think is better: buying houses for $25,000 each with average down payments of $2,000 and, after fix-up, rents of $400 per month, or houses that cost $60,000 each with $10,000 cash down payments and rents of $550 per month? If you own both kinds right now, you already know which are best. If you don't know the answer yet, by all means study the numbers before you invest. Just remember, cash flow means survival; the opposite spells disaster.

How Much Risk Is Too Much?

Once I decided where I wanted my plan to take me and chose inexpensive fix-up houses as the vehicle to get me there, I then considered how much risk would be involved. Shopping centers and special-use buildings are high-risk properties, as is vacant land. Land speculation is like gambling. Bare land can sit for years without generating any income or payback. Special-use buildings like airport hangars, bowling alleys, auto factories, and resorts can sink an investor quickly if the tenant moves out. You limit yourself to a very specialized group of tenants when you own special-use properties. It's dangerous for beginners who normally don't have holding power (extra cash reserves). Full-time investors and career changers who need immediate cash flow must select the right kind of properties to make it happen. Most properties are not candidates.

In my own case, I knew from the very beginning that I could not stand many vacancies. Obviously, too much risk of any sort was not what I wanted or needed. Just imagine how long you could last if you owned a see-through office building in Houston. Some buildings have stood there for years with little or no rents coming in. Many wealthy guys have joined the ranks of poor folks with no income to pay hefty mortgage payments. By the way, see-through means that you can look straight through those fancy glass windows to the other side. With no tenants, you have a perfect unobstructed view. That, my friends, is what I call high-risk investing. Forget that kind if you're just getting started.

My good friend, Bill Nickerson, spent his entire investment career specializing in fix-up (adding value). His efforts made him a very wealthy man. Bill admitted he was sometimes tempted to invest in the more glamorous properties. Once he got fast-talked into buying a beautiful resort property that worked him silly, but made very little money. Bill never again veered from fixer-uppers. Stay with run-down, fixer-upper types of properties. Buy them at a discount, and then improve the value. Always fight off the temptation to make a quick buck with a risky investment that sounds too good to be true. Chances are, it is.

An ideal long-term plan should include a combination of properties in order to reduce risk and maximize earnings. Some, such as rental units, should produce cash flow almost immediately, and others, such as medium-priced houses, should generally have greater appreciation potential. It's always much easier to obtain loan funds using single-family houses as collateral. Combination plans will tag all the bases. You'll have multi-unit properties with cash flow, plus single houses for long-term appreciation.

Always Invest Where Demand Is Highest

It's very important to stay within your means financially and to acquire the type of properties you can personally handle your-self. If you do that, you can almost eliminate the risk factor. Inexpensive rental houses and small apartment buildings will always have long waiting lists of qualified tenants if you keep the properties looking attractive and in good repair.

According to HUD, 50,000 lower-income rental units are disappearing in this country annually. They are torn down for urban expansion, turned into condos, or just fall down. The reason doesn't matter much. The point is that they're becoming as scarce as hens' teeth. First thing you know, the federal government might start subsidizing landlords who own what's left. Certainly that would make as much sense as paying farmers to plow their tomatoes under so they don't flood the market and bring the prices down.

Because they are scarce and in such high demand, the risk of owning and operating inexpensive rental houses is almost nonexistent. That's exactly what new investors need—nonexistent risk. There are plenty of other things to worry about, like selecting the right tenants. We'll save that for later.

The Best Odds for Your Success

Bill Nickerson, author and fix-up millionaire, began fixing rental houses over 50 years ago. Bill quite accurately concludes in his best-selling book, *How I Turned $1,000 into Three Million in My Spare Time*, "The chance for success is 1600 times better owning and operating rental properties than for starting another type of business." If you need more convincing, I suggest you write to the Bank of America Business Services Department or Dun & Bradstreet's Credit Rating Services, Inc. The information they provide about starting other businesses and the odds for success are quite gloomy by comparison.

When You're Ready to Buy

When you're ready to buy a fixer-upper property, the first thing you should do is develop your marketing plan. For fix-and-sell investing, you must determine how much you can sell the fixed-up property for (fair market value). If your plan is to rent, you must know—before you actually purchase the property—how much rent you will get when the property is fixed. Don't buy the property first and then wonder how much you can get later. Know how much you can get first. Then you will know exactly how much money you can spend buying the property and fixing it up. For example, I always plan on a minimum of 15 percent annual return on my fixed-up rental houses. Don't include appreciation or tax savings in this computation. My return is based on the total fix-up cost of the property. If I buy a house for

$44,000 and spend $6,000 for fix-up, that means I must get $625 per month rent ($44,000 + $6,000 = $50,000 x 15% = $7,500 annually). If your plan is to sell and you wish to earn a minimum 15-percent profit, you should work the numbers backwards from the market price.

For example, let's say the $44,000 house I purchase is 20 percent below current market value. That means the fixed-up value will be $55,000. I plan to do the work myself; however, material costs will be about $2,000 or roughly one-third of the $6,000 total fix-up estimate. In this example, the $44,000 cost plus the $2,000 fix-up = $46,000 completed. If I sell at market value ($55,000), my gross profit will be $9,000, which exceeds my minimum profit expectations.

I cannot overemphasize the importance of learning values in your buying area. This means sales values, rent values, and of course, the cost of doing the fix-up work (materials and labor). At my seminars and fixer-upper camps, I teach students how to develop their own chart showing various rent levels and the likely purchase price of properties based on their income and location. You must know what properties should cost and what they will reasonably sell for. Do this exercise before you buy, not afterwards.

A Good Plan Requires Action

Once you have developed your financial success plan—you've decided where you wish to go, chosen the vehicle to get you there, and selected an investment with the lowest possible risk based on your personal resources and abilities, you've completed the first step. Now you are ready to implement your plan.

Don't wait until you know everything about investing. You never will. Investment education comes mostly from investing.

Obviously, you must learn all you can from reading, class-rooms, and seminars. However, unless you actually do some investing yourself, you'll be missing the most important part of the learning process.

The single, most dangerous roadblock facing every career-changer and full-time wannabe is procrastination. There is no doubt that many folks with the best intentions and even a good workable plan will procrastinate forever. Remember, financial success is not a stroke of luck. It involves a solid workable plan and working the plan. The success part comes automatically when you do the things I've suggested. It's time to start right now.

3

Building Success One Brick at a Time

In this chapter you will learn about:

- The power of cash flow
- Multiplying your assets and net worth
- Becoming an expert and knowing your rental market
- The four sources of profits in real estate

Investing in houses, at the right price, is a good, solid business opportunity that can make you financially independent. Houses aren't glamorous like shopping malls or high-tech commercial buildings, and you'll never be the center of attention at cocktail parties yapping about your tenants, but there are important trade-offs that are much better suited to investors like me, who start with very little cash and no reserves.

To begin with, it doesn't take a whole lot of time and training before you'll be able to start buying investment properties and make a little money doing it. It won't seem like much at first, but gradually, as you improve your buying skills, a silent but powerful helper called *compounding* shows up to assist you. Compounding works two different ways. First, it works with the passage of time to multiply your assets and increase your net worth. Second, as you learn more and more about investing, your brain (ideas) begins to compound too. As your knowledge expands, you will begin to visualize exciting new opportunities with great potential for making money. The results—your profits will increase with each new idea. Both kinds of compounding are very powerful tools when it comes to building your personal wealth, believe me.

Never underestimate the power of making small profits consistently. You don't need killer deals to make yourself wealthy. What you need are the right properties that will earn you money on a regular basis, preferably monthly. A solid brick house, built to last for centuries, always begins construction with the first layer of bricks. Properly laid, these first bricks will provide the strong underlying foundation to support the entire house. Building strong real estate investments starts out exactly the same way—one layer of bricks at a time. It will pay for you to concentrate on execution rather than speed. Making sure you earn a little profit on each new property you acquire is a far better strategy than going for the whole enchilada on a super deal. That's the way most of the rich folks got rich—just one brick at a time.

Ray Kroc, founder of McDonald's, consistently sold hamburgers and French fries for 15 cents each from 1955, when he started, until 1967. He then raised his prices to 18 cents. That certainly doesn't sound like a high-roller operation, but when you keep repeating a winning formula, even small numbers add up to big bucks. When Mr. Kroc retired from McDonald's and bought the San Diego Padre's baseball team in 1974, just 19 years after serving up his first batch of fries, his personal net worth exceeded $400 million. That's a potful of zeroes for just peddling 15-cent hamburgers with fries.

Beware Future Value, High Potential, and Pride of Ownership

After years of trying many different strategies to make money with real estate, I can tell you without the slightest hiccup that it's not a sound idea to buy houses that don't "pencil out" on the day you acquire them or shortly thereafter. There's only one good reason in the world I know of to buy income properties—to make money. If the houses won't do that or can't, then I don't want them regardless of whatever else I think about them.

I have been sucked in on future value, high potential, and pride of ownership so many times, I'm embarrassed to admit it. Fortunately for me, I learned my hardest lessons early in my career before I had a ton of money to lose.

If your goals are something like mine—investing for current income and long-term security, with the least amount of daily management involvement—then my strategies will work well for you. Naturally, there are many things to learn and most of them should be learned during the early stages of your investing. On-the-job training is most important.

Don't Let Big Mortgage Payments Rob Your Profits

When you acquire properties with financing, which most of us do, you should always insist on long-term paybacks. The longer, the better but nothing less than 10 years. Be very careful when you agree on the amount of the mortgage payments. In my opinion, investment properties that have mortgage payments of more than 55 percent of the scheduled income are a bit too risky, unless, of course, you have additional resources to pay for negative cash flow. I'm quite satisfied when my mortgaged properties earn me a small cash profit consistently every month. Small profits allow me to buy additional properties, which in turn provide more small profits. First thing you know, my small profits, added together, turn into big profits!

Walt Disney was delighted with the opportunity to draw the first animated cartoons shown on big theater screens. He was paid only $12 apiece for each one, but he kept cranking drawings out, faster and faster. Needless to say, the $12 drawings added up quickly and made Disney a very wealthy man. Naturally, it didn't happen overnight, but when you consistently keep small profits rolling in, you have the money to move toward bigger and better opportunities as they present themselves.

Become an Expert to Stay on Top

Even if you have a few dollars in reserve, you must never forget a basic principal of wealth building: You never get very rich writing checks. It's deposits that will get you there. I often refer to my rental houses as widgets, because it sounds more like I'm in a business, as opposed to being a real estate investor. Investors, especially do-it-yourself folks who follow my advice, need to think a whole lot more like business people, in my opinion.

Business people market products (such as widgets) at competitive prices for the purpose of earning themselves reasonable profits for their efforts. Business people must become experts at figuring their cost of inventory, overhead, and payroll expenses. If they don't, they quickly go out of business.

I continually get telephone calls from real estate investors who purchase properties without even the foggiest idea of how much money it will cost for fix-up and repairs. Many have no idea what I'm even talking about when I ask them, "How much money do you expect the property will pay you back?" I must confess, I have a great deal of optimism and just plain blind faith when it comes to real estate investing, but I certainly don't want to own houses that force me to reach in my wallet every month to pay for cash shortages. That's the wrong direction for building personal wealth.

Your ability to make money in the real estate business will depend more on you than on the property. The property is the vehicle. However, it's your skills that must produce the cash. For example, if you don't know exactly how much money it costs to operate rental units but you guess that 30 to 35 percent of gross rents should be enough, what happens if it actually costs 45 to 50 percent instead? Let's assume you thought that 35 percent for expenses was the right amount and you structured the monthly mortgage payment at 60 percent of the monthly income. If you are correct, you will have 5 percent of gross rents left over to keep for yourself. However, can you see the dilemma if your expenses turn out to be 45 percent of gross income instead? Now you have a serious problem with basic math. $45\% + 60\% =$ too much! Beyond the simple math issue, the more serious problem is the fact the 5 percent error will cost you money, rather than earn money for you.

At least once every year investors need to sit down at the kitchen table with a big yellow writing pad and plot out exactly where they're headed, where they've been, and, equally important, whether they're still on course to get where they'd like to be. You'd be amazed at the number of folks I talk to who don't have the slightest notion whether or not they're headed in the right direction. It should certainly come as no surprise. If you don't know where you're going, it's almost impossible to tell when and where you'll end up. That's far too much uncertainty in my opinion.

Know Your Rental Market

Nearly every city and town across the country where people buy or rent housing is a good location for fix-up investing. The reason that locations are less important than you might think is because you must plan your investment strategy to meet the needs of a specific customer. First, you must always determine if you can make a profit renting or selling. You must do this *before* you purchase any property. If the numbers work out in the plus column, it doesn't matter too much where you invest. As you might well imagine, there is definitely a home-field advantage to investing where you live because you are more likely to know the local market prices best where you live. Also, doing business, setting up trade accounts, and banking are always easier at home.

Never underestimate the importance of knowing your marketplace. It's the key factor to buying. It makes little sense to have a $100,000 house for sale in a town filled with $75,000 buyers. The same thing goes for renting. It makes for a very poor rental operation if you purchase $100,000 houses in a town where 90 percent of your potential tenants work at Kmart and Burger King. They simply can't afford your product.

I have found tenants who are paying $500 in rent for a $400 house. When you see the tenants, you'll often understand why. In one particular case, only four occupants were listed on the rental agreement, but I counted 12 people coming out the door one morning, about 9 A.M., while I was snooping around on the property. Sometimes you can get a good idea about who lives at a place by checking out the cars parked on the property after dark. When I sense that negotiations to purchase a property are going my way, I spend extra time driving by and observing what goes on at the property. The best word that describes how I conduct these observations is *sneaky*. No calling ahead like most real estate agents do for a staged visit. You can't really learn what's happening unless you sneak around a bit.

If you plan to rent your properties to regular, everyday tenants at prevailing market rents, you must find out exactly what those rents are. You can do this by matching the rents in classified ads to comparable properties in the same neighborhood as yours (or soon to be yours). Some valuable information can be learned from this exercise. First, you will learn whether the rents are too high or low for the property you are negotiating to purchase. Hopefully, they're low, so you'll be able to raise them. Equally important for your education is that you'll discover the right amount of income for the property. When you know exactly what the true market income should be for a particular property, it becomes relatively easy to figure out what you can pay for it and still make a profit on the deal.

A Word of Caution About Seaside Cities

Let me add another comment about where to invest or, more importantly, where not to invest. Cities by the ocean are generally very expensive locations. Competition is tough, and start-up costs are often beyond the means of average folks. In particular, start-out investors have very little cash in the bank. In a seller's market, which is almost always the case in large seaside cities, it seems that cash buyers are standing on every street corner. A great number of these folks have more money than brains. I've often wondered how they got it. But my point is that they have the juice to bid up prices. Trying to do business in this environment is like playing poker with Donald Trump. The odds are far too high against regular folks.

My advice is to drop back inland 50 miles or so where you can't feel the ocean breeze in your face or smell saltwater. You'll find properties for half the price or less. Remember what investing is really about. It's about making money now. Don't confuse investing with speculating for some big pot of gold in the future. You'll end up broke long before the pot ever shows up. It's called fool's gold, and they named it that for a good reason.

There Is No Substitute for Cash Flow

Over the years I have constantly invested my money (sometimes very little) and my personal energies in the kinds of properties that would earn me a profit every month. Often my profits didn't amount to much, but my basic strategy of investing for a steady monthly income has always served me well. When properties generate cash flow, you always have money in your pockets. It may not even be positive cash flow during bad months, but it's still money that's paid to you as a property owner. Therefore, it's you who gets to decide how much to keep and how much to pay out every month. Cash flow is very important for your long-term financial health.

It's said that possession is nine-tenths of the law. In the rental housing business we call this MIF (money in the fist). It's very important to control the money. Money is like gasoline for your airplane. As long as you have it, you'll keep right on flying. Without it, you'll crash and burn. This is one of the biggest problems I have with fixing up houses and then waiting for a qualified buyer to come along and bail me out. My money is tied up in the house while mortgage payments, taxes, and insurance drain my bank account. New investors call this flipping. (When I started out, flipping meant something else.)

I have learned from experience that cash flow is much easier to achieve when you're buying small, multiple properties, such as three or four houses on a single lot, or several duplexes with a house or two. I call these various combinations *leper properties.* I own many properties with five to eight living units each. They become excellent cash flow producers after a year or so. My goal to accomplish a turnaround (total fix-up job) is 18 to 24 months. There are many good financial reasons why I favor keeping a flock of rental houses, but the reason dearest to me is that they furnish me with a pocketful of cash every month, come rain or shine. Over the years, as the mortgages are retired (paid off), I have extra cash on hand to buy discounted mortgages, including buying back my own debt. It's a very lucrative companion business to my real estate investing.

In my opinion, nothing comes ahead of cash flow. If you have it, you will continue to grow. You can transition from smaller properties to larger ones or fixer-uppers to pride-of-ownership. You can use your cash flow to buy mortgages for passive income or take a trip around the world every month when the rents come in. Cash flow gives you many choices. When you own the houses, you have your own personal money machine. Obviously, you must maintain the property and provide the necessary management, but in exchange for doing this, you control the money. It's yours to spend any way you choose. Owning your own widgets is the surest path to financial independence. The basis for nearly all wealth can be traced to the ownership of a patent, copyright, or grant deed. Owning income-producing real estate puts you smack dab in the middle of the right crowd.

Four Sources of Real Estate Profits

Real estate profits come from four primary sources:

1. Cash flow from rents
2. Equity build-up amortization
3. Tax shelters (saving income)
4. Appreciation (growth)

Let's examine how each one of these works.

Cash Flow

Cash flow is fairly easy to figure out. It's simply all the income your assets generate. For example, if your rental house takes in $500 per month from rents, then the cash flow is $6,000 annually (12 x $500 = $6,000).

There are two kinds of cash flow: positive and negative. Using the example above, if you take in $6,000 annually from rents but spend $7,000 a year operating the property, the net result is $1,000 negative cash flow. Obviously, positive cash flow is the kind we're seeking. We want net income, meaning the amount of cash flow left over after paying all the expenses needed to operate the property.

Equity Build-Up

Equity build-up or amortization is the reduction in mortgage balance you owe each time you make a mortgage payment. For most real estate loans, the principal amount you owe each month after you make your payment goes down by just a smidgen (not much). For example, if your amortized loan payment is $1,000 per month, the interest on the loan might cost $950 of the payment, which leaves only $50 to reduce the principal balance. If the principal balance was $90,000 before the payment, then it's only $89,950 afterwards. The equity build-up would be $50 for the month. Annually, it might be closer to $700 since each month just a little more of the total monthly payment goes toward principal reduction. Principal reduction is the part that reduces your mortgage balance.

Tax Shelters

Tax shelters result from losing money—but there are good losses and bad losses, similar to cholesterol in your bloodstream. You have your good cholesterol called HDL and the bad cholesterol called LDL.

Tax shelters that result from spending hard dollars are a lot like LDL cholesterol. You don't want more than necessary. What you do want are the kinds of tax shelter that don't cost hard dollars. The way you get this kind is from property depreciation. Depreciation is the "wearing out" of an income-producing asset. The tax code allows a bookkeeping reduction in the value of a property each year as the asset wears out. For example, if your $1,000 carpet wears out in five years, the depreciation expense or allowance is $200 worth of wearing out each year. You don't spend $200 each year, but you can deduct a $200 loss from the rent money just the same as if you had spent $200 (real dollars) fixing the toilet.

Bad tax shelters are the kind where you spend hard dollars to get them. Many inexperienced investors seem quite content with LDL-type shelters. Spending $100 to get $50 back is not a good strategy. It's like buying a new car because you want new seat covers and tires. In rare cases, spending extra hard dollars to generate tax losses might make some sense, but not too often.

Ideally, what you want is a property that shelters its own rental income with its own depreciation expense deduction and even has some loss left over to shelter additional income from another source, like from your paycheck working at the sawmill. Table 3-1 shows a simple example of what I mean.

Since nobody had to pay the $4,000 depreciation, it's really just a bookkeeping expense. By counting just the real expenses, you can see that they too only add up to $10,000 worth of checks to write. In reality, there's a $2,000 bottom line profit. For tax reporting, however, the property still shows a $2,000 loss, even though we get to put $2,000 hard cash in our pocket. Not only that, but this tax loss is extra. It can be used to offset or reduce the taxes on $2,000 worth of positive income from your paycheck at the sawmill. For example, if you earn $20,000

Annual Income		$ Amount
Total Income from Rents		$12,000
Annual Expenses	**$ Amount**	
Taxes	1,200	
Insurance	600	
Management	1,000	
Maintenance	1,400	
Utilities	460	
Services	340	
Total Cash Expenses		$5,000
Total Depreciation (noncash expenses)		4,000
Total Interest Expense on Mortgage		5,000
Total Income or Loss		($2,000)

Table 3-1. How investing in property shelters income

this year at the sawmill, the $2,000 property loss will allow you to report only $18,000 for tax purposes. If you pay 30 cents out of each dollar in taxes, you've just earned (or saved) $600 on your paycheck. That means you get the $600 in addition to the $2,000 you already pocketed from the property. Ain't these tax-sheltering properties grand?

In the above example, let's say the mortgage is too big or has a very high interest rate and the interest expenses for the year are $10,000 instead of $5,000. Now the bottom line shows a $7,000 loss. You still get the same $4,000 depreciation expenses; however, now you've lost the $2,000 profit you got to put in your pocket before. Not only that, but you also must feed the property an extra $3,000 because that's how much the real cash expenses exceed the income. You can still use the $7,000 loss to reduce the taxable income from your paycheck, but at 30 cents per dollar it's worth only $2,100. The net result of this situation would be a real cash loss of $900, as opposed to $2,600 profit in the first example. Paying too much for properties is the main culprit. But remember, you can have similar results from abnormally high expenses.

Appreciation

Appreciation happens when prices are driven up for a variety of reasons. Some say deficit spending by the government is the reason. But whatever the causes real estate prices almost always go up. It doesn't mean the houses will actually be worth more in the future. It does mean that they'll cost more. Obviously when you're the owner, you'll receive more when you sell them.

Several friends of mine purchased single-family homes in southern California during the late 1950s for $26,500. Thirty years later they sold them for $350,000. The houses didn't improve after 30 years of use. The prices were simply driven up by inflation in the marketplace. It's called supply and demand. Obviously, the purchasing power of a dollar shrank considerably during the 30-year period. Still, in terms of plain old profits, my friends made $323,500 by simply owning and living in their houses that long. That's the same thing as being paid $10,800 for each year of ownership. I'll be the first to admit, markets like Los Angeles don't exist everywhere, but appreciation in the 5-percent range is not at all uncommon. Five-percent appreciation, compounded over 30 years, will add substantial value to real estate holdings.

So far I'm talking about appreciation that results from natural causes. Forced inflation or appreciation is a whole different ballgame. It occurs because investors like myself make it happen—and with forced appreciation we're not stuck with any piddly 5-percent annual increase. Fifty percent is much more like it. Forced appreciation results from doing something to increase the value of real estate. Fixing run-down properties automatically forces the values up. Straightening out lousy management and improving poor rent collections do the same. It's not the least bit uncommon to purchase pigsty-looking properties for 30 to 50 percent under what normal market prices would be if they were well-performing properties; that is, fixed up and sparkling clean. Forced appreciation is the biggest profit maker and the fastest way to build wealth for most do-it-yourself investors. Forced appreciation, along with cash flow from rents and tax savings, can produce investor returns unequaled by any other wealth-building formulas I know of.

4

Magic Ingredients for a Moneymaking Plan

In this chapter you will learn about:

- The best time to buy and sell
- The best way to create equity
- Ideal financing terms to make a profit
- The heart of wealth-building: education and action

Every time I start talking about making profits at my seminars, someone always reminds me that all one needs to do is buy properties wholesale and sell them at retail. You can't help but admire the genius behind such advice, but I often wonder—doesn't the asker realize that this is what we're all trying to do? The big problem is that buying low and selling high is not all that easy to do. In fact, it takes some really sound profit engineering to develop a moneymaking strategy. A good plan must have several common ingredients, such as proper timing, equity creation, good financing, and a reasonable method to extract the profits. None of these can be left to chance if you intend to make any serious money investing in real estate.

My rental houses provide me with a reliable income and allow me time to market my properties without being under the gun. There's a tremendous disadvantage in having to sell when you need the money to live as opposed to having all the time you need to handpick your buyer. Being able to wait for Mr. Right can often be worth 20 to 40 percent more than settling for whatever comes along. Therefore, my standing advice is to buy a few good rental properties to start with. Get a monthly income established so that you never look hungry when you're selling. Buyers can smell a starving seller a mile away.

Almost anyone with a reasonable amount of knowledge can buy decent middle-class tract houses for a little bit less than what they are appraised for. The biggest problem is buying them cheaply enough so that you'll be able to sell or rent them for a profit. If you pay 10 percent less than the asking price of $85,000 for a house and you can rent the place for only $100 more than the mortgage payment, you'll quickly run out of down payments and your investment plan will soon be stuck in the mud. Selling for a profit anytime soon is not very likely because you're basically playing the appreciation game. About the only way you could extract any profits is to wait until the property goes up in value or to keep making payments until the mortgage is paid down. Either way, it's not an exciting plan, even if the house is a good, sound investment.

No Cash Down Means No Profits

Many neophyte investors have made the mistake of buying marked-up houses for no money down. They automatically assumed they could earn a profit somehow, because no cash was invested. With high mortgage payments and short-term balloon notes, their dreams of becoming tycoons quickly turned to nightmares instead. The free-lunch strategy may work well for selling slick-covered books on cable TV, but in the real world you won't buy much value for nothing.

The important thing to remember is that you can purchase properties with dollars or pay with your personal skills, but you must always pay. When you are negotiating to buy a property, stop and think about the deal as if you were the seller. Would you sell your real estate for nothing down if you thought someone would make a normal down payment? In most cases, acquiring properties for no money down means you're paying too much to start with. That's the wrong way to make profits in this business.

The Poor Investor's Plan for Profits

Buying for cash is one way you can get big discounts, especially in a buyer's market. With good knowledge about your buying area, it's not too difficult to purchase $100,000 houses for $80,000–$85,000 cash. Every time you do it, you'll make $15,000–$20,000 at closing. Five or six deals a year will earn you $100,000 profits, plus $4,000 in monthly income. With cash flow and tax savings, you'll likely earn 15 to 20 percent annually. And, with appreciation, the percentage is even higher. It's a good sound plan. It's safe and offers excellent earnings to investors who have the cash. If you're not quite ready to pay cash just yet, then it's absolutely necessary that you learn an alternative strategy for profit-making. I call mine "The Poor Investor's Plan for Profits." It utilizes each one of the ingredients I mention earlier. It's also a bit more complicated than buying for cash. But, if you do it right, you'll end up just as wealthy as the investors who had money to start with. Here are the ingredients for the Poor Investor's Plan for Profits.

Proper Timing

To maximize profits you must buy houses when it seems like the wrong thing to do. Buying during a buyer's market (that's when many properties are available with very few interested buyers) is generally worth at least a 15-percent discount to those who have the guts to go against the flow. For example, an $80,000 property should sell for $68,000 without much haggling. Conversely, during a seller's market (opposite of a buyer's market), the same $80,000 house will likely fetch + $92,000 (15 percent more).

As you can see, being synchronized with the up-and-down real estate cycles can be worth $24,000 when you understand there's a right time to buy and there's a right time to sell. If you follow the crowd, you'll likely end up doing exactly the opposite of what I'm suggesting here. To prove my point, try to find someone you know in the crowd who is rich. I'll bet you can't find a single person. When major newspapers and financial reports begin recommending real estate investing to the public, shrewd owners immediately quit buying and polish up their properties to sell for maximum prices to crowds of dummies who will happily pay whatever the market will bear. Remember, the $24,000 price difference we're discussing here has nothing to do with adding value or appreciation. You earn the money by simply buying and selling at the proper time.

Forced Equity Creation

When you purchase average properties in average condition, you can expect to pay average prices and terms. Equity creation or build-up comes from two sources. The first is very insignificant. It's the principal portion of each mortgage payment, which adds to equity in the property with each monthly payment. The second kind is what I do. It's called *adding value*. It comes from fixing up a property or straightening out people problems by initiating better management. This kind of equity is forced equity. The owner makes it happen.

One of the best ways to create equity is to improve the financial performance (raising rents) of a property. For example, if I'm able to fix up a run-down property and increase rents from $20,000 to $30,000 annually, that's forced equity creation. If the property is worth eight times the gross rents, I've increased the value from $160,000 to $240,000—that's an $80,000 equity addition. It has nothing to do with normal appreciation. It was forced to increase by my fix-up work. If the building appreciates by 5 percent next year, that will add $12,000 equity to the $80,000 I've created.

Good Financing

Unless you're a cash buyer, good financing is absolutely essential to earning big profits. If you can't offer decent financing when you decide to sell, you'll end up making concessions to the buyer, which will greatly reduce your potential profits. What I do and recommend for you is to mentally sell your property at the same time you are negotiating to buy it. In other words, think ahead to when and how you plan to market the property someday in the future—that is, specifically the kind of financing you'll be able to offer your buyer in the future. If you agree to mortgages that cannot be assumed (due-on-sale clause), you'll restrict any future sales to a buyer who must qualify for new financing. If you agree to short-term notes or mortgages, most buyers will balk at assuming them. High mortgage payments are also restrictive because buyers are concerned about cash flow.

The best kind of financing you can offer when it comes to making a future sale is a long-term (20 to 30 years) seller carry-back mortgage with the following characteristics: no due-on-sale provision, payments that are 50 percent or less of the current rental income, and a reasonable interest rate. This type of mortgage can easily be wrapped (wrap-around) with a new all-inclusive mortgage allowing the seller to earn extra profits on the interest spread, which reduces the income tax burden caused by installment reporting.

Ruth B: A Case for Buying Rental Units and Keeping Them

Several years back I purchased four small duplexes from the estate of Ruth B. (not her real name). Ruth had passed away at age 88, leaving the property to a young niece who had taken care of her aunt in later years. She also helped her with the rental units. I learned from the niece that Ruth had owned the duplexes for nearly 50 years. She and her late husband, Bill, had bought them while he was working for the railroad. Their idea back then was to invest for retirement. Obviously, neither could have predicted that Ruth would outlive her husband by almost 19 years. The duplexes were Ruth's sole source of support with the exception of a small pension check of less than $300 per month. By comparison, the duplexes were renting for $325 each or a total monthly income of $2,600 when I bought them. I estimated that rents were at least $50 under the market value at the time I acquired them.

The reason I pass along this story is to show you an everyday real-life example of how real estate investing pays off for those who search out the right kind of properties. I'm sure Ruth and her husband had dreams of enjoying the extra income during their retirement, perhaps to pursue hobbies, take some trips together, or even buy a frill or two. Most certainly, their main goal, I'm sure, was a comfortable retirement when Bill's railroading days were over. In this case, as so often happens, fate had a way of rearranging the best laid plans. Retirement for Ruth and her husband wasn't meant to last very long, but the benefits from their duplex ownership would. For 19 years Ruth's life was considerably more comfortable because of their wise decision made many years before. The $2,600 monthly rents that Ruth enjoyed make a pretty good case for buying rental units and keeping them.

Real Estate Requires Your Total Concentration

As I said already, don't do anything until you sit down and figure out what you wish to accomplish. If you don't do this, you're likely to get your investment cart before the horse. It's impossible to achieve any kind of success if you don't know where you're going. Also, let me mention skipping around. If you keep skipping around, looking for greener pastures or a better mousetrap, chances are you'll never do well with real estate. Real estate investing requires your total concentration and a specific game plan or goal. Diversions will only slow your progress and delay any success you might achieve. Don't waste your time thinking nonsense like there's some way you can make a lot of money in the real estate business without first learning the ropes. Education and action are the magic words. Trying to skip education or looking for an easy way simply won't work. You'd be better off soaking in the bathtub playing with a rubber duck if you think you can make big bucks without paying your dues.

Keep It Simple

Any plan should be kept very simple when you first start out. Naturally, it can become more sophisticated as you go along. If you're like me, you will continually be making adjustments and revisions as you learn new and better strategies. The key point to remember here is keep things simple until you're smart and knowledgeable enough to make profitable changes. Although my investment plan has been revised many times over the years, it was a very basic idea when I started. Let me share a few of the thoughts I had back then.

To start with, I had made up my mind to change careers. I knew I couldn't do it overnight, so I planned to make it happen in three years. As things turned out it took me only two years. I had a regular job, but I knew that, once I left it, I would need a new source of income. That meant I would need to buy the kind of real estate that would quickly generate positive cash flow during the following three years. Obviously, the biggest question I had back then was "What kind of property can I purchase that will provide me with a solid income in just three year's time?" The answer might have been easier if I'd had more money, but the fact was I didn't. Looking back now, I feel quite fortunate that I was able to tap my telephone company savings plan for the small down payment on the property on Pine Street. Pine Street was my first fixer-upper property in Redding, California. It was four houses on a single lot.

Biggest Profits Come from Small, Affordable, Multi-Unit Properties

When I look back at what I've accomplished, I can tell you that my fastest cash flow and biggest profits have always come from small, affordable, multiple-unit properties. One perfect example was my Hillcrest Cottages. Hillcrest was a 50-year-old motor lodge. I fixed it up and converted it to 22 senior rental apartments. Basically, I paid no money down when I acquired the property for $234,000. I sold it less than two years later for $435,000.

Another group of 11 run-down houses on a single-acre lot earned me $150,000 for just over a year's fix-up work. That sale brought me a $50,000 cash down payment. My eight fixer-upper houses on Adam Way were renting for only $1,680 when I acquired them. Today they rent for $4,330. When your rents increase and your biggest single expense, the mortgage payment, stays the same, it doesn't take a rocket scientist to figure out that you're making serious money for your efforts. Remember what I told you earlier—education and action are the magic ingredients. There is simply no way you can be successful investing in real estate unless you learn about what you're doing and continually practice the things you learn. The real secret to success is being ready for opportunity when it arrives. There are quite a number of folks with a few dollars in their pockets all primed and ready to invest in something, but, unfortunately for many, they could walk right past the gold mine without ever knowing it because they lack enough knowledge to spot value, even when they're standing in the middle of it.

People who purchase my books and tape courses often ask, "Do you think your $49 book will teach me enough, or do you think it will take the more expensive $395 study course to do the trick?" One fella bought my book instead of my tape album because he needed the money to attend a concert featuring the Doobie Brothers. Unfortunately, I can't compete with that. I have never yet known or been around a successful person in real estate or anything else who wasn't constantly trying to learn more and improve himself or herself. I have owned and managed more than 200 houses filled with all kinds of tenants, and I'm still interested in learning more about real estate and management. I know that's the reason I've been successful with my houses. Basketball great Larry Bird says, "If you don't do your homework, you won't make your freethrows." Same goes for making opportunities.

5

12 Benefits to Being a Housing Entrepreneur

In this chapter you will learn about:

- Tax deductions to take as you set up your business
- How depreciation puts money in your pocket
- Setting up a forced savings plan
- Creating a retirement nest egg

If I asked you to choose between being a rich garbage collector and a poor apartment owner, which would you choose? I'm not conducting a survey here, but my gut feeling is, you'd pick rich garbage collector. That's my answer too! Had the choices been between a rich garbage collector and rich apartment owner, then I'd switch back to apartment owner. If you think like me, rich is the first choice. My plan to get there has some flexibility. Obviously, I love real estate investing, but I'll be first to admit that the money has an awful lot to do with my love affair. It's been my long-term observation that people who invest in real estate are not much different from those who invest in pizza parlors or buy carpet-cleaning trucks. The reason this is so, I think, is because the motivation factors are exactly alike. Industrious folks are constantly looking for ways to get ahead financially and improve the quality of their lives. Many are highly motivated to leave traditional 9-to-5 jobs for an opportunity to work for themselves. Of course, it goes without saying that most of us have a desire to end up financially independent once our working days are over.

I often tell my students at seminars, "I don't mind workin' extra hard and for long hours if the anticipated rewards are proportional to my efforts." Over the years my rental business has met all my early expectations and exceeded many. Once you get this business up and running, you'll quickly find out, as I have, that the rewards are nearly unbeatable.

Following are 12 major benefits you'll enjoy as a housing entrepreneur. As you read each one, compare it to whatever benefits you might be receiving now. How do my benefits stack up against yours?

1. Monthly Cash Flow

There are a variety of different ways to increase cash flow in the investment housing business, depending on how you choose to start out. In case you missed it before, one cash flow generator I used when I was first starting out was to manage houses for other investors. I also did fix-up work and received compensation from the owners. Sometimes I was allowed to keep the cash after paying all the expenses. When I upgraded the properties, I would often try to negotiate options to purchase a half interest. I would also receive finder's fees for locating good deals. Finder's fees, compensation for my fix-up work, and keeping cash from rents after expenses were paid do not require a real estate license, which I didn't have.

Another technique I used when I became more experienced was my 90/10 Cash Investor Plan, detailed in my book *Investing in Fixer-Uppers*. These methods all generate income, but my primary moneymaking strategy has been adding value to real estate (fixing up run-down houses). You can buy them more cheaply with more liberal terms (better financing) once you learn a few negotiating skills. All it takes is practice. It's by far the quickest way to earn big profits in the real estate business.

Common sense will tell you that sellers of ugly houses receive fewer offers for their properties than sellers of great-looking properties. This is especially true in locations where a good selection of decent houses are for sale. Often the sellers of ugly houses become lonely and feel rejected. Finally they become desperate to hear a buyer's voice. This situation creates a very favorable shopping opportunity for buyers of ugly houses who have the know-how to solve a lonely seller's dilemma. Negotiating a good price and terms are the biggest differences between investors who build large monthly cash flows and those who need a second job so they can buy more real estate. Renting $100,000 houses for $700 per month won't make you rich anytime soon. Renting $30,000 houses for $600 will. It's simply a matter of learning which properties you can purchase at wholesale prices so that you can operate on a positive cash flow basis just like any other successful business. Once you're rich, it's OK to diversify and buy nice-looking, sweet-smelling houses. After all, money's not everything.

2. You Can Work at Home

Consider how much less complicated your life would be if your office were your own kitchen table. No freeways, no babysitters, and no strict time schedules to follow. My kitchen table is still my center of operations after doing house fix-up investing for many years, although, as I've mentioned, I did have to add a new center leaf when I needed more room to count rent money. When you decide to become a housing entrepreneur on a full-time basis, naturally your home can be your office since it's much more convenient than working outside your home. As such, you may claim full tax deductions for the part of your house you use to operate your business. That means house payments, utility bills, yard care—everything! This could easily split your housing costs in half. You pay half, and your rental operation pays the other half. Certainly this is a big advantage for beginners so they don't have the extra expense of a regular office. I would suggest a separate telephone number with a recorder and caller ID to be used for business calls. Later on, you may wish to operate a separate rental office away from home when you have enough tenants to justify the expense.

3. Maximum Tax Savings

When you work for yourself, in any business, lots of ordinary expenses become tax-deductible business expenses. Your car is a good example. You must pay for a car that you drive to work and to the store with your net (after tax) take-home paycheck. That is *not* the way you get rich. In the rental housing business, your transportation is a business expense. It gets paid for from income (before taxes), not after. That's a big dollar difference, as you will see.

By far the most powerful tax deductions you'll enjoy come from the depreciation of rental houses. Depreciation is subtracted from rental income, just the same as fixing toilets, except that it doesn't cost you anything, like the plumbing bill would. For example, a house with annual depreciation of

$4,800 would allow you to keep $400 per month rent income without paying one thin dime in taxes.

The ability to use all your money for the purpose of buying additional assets (houses) rather than mailing a check to the IRS is one of the main reasons real estate investing makes you lots richer than folks who earn W-2 wages without tax deductions. Rental housing income is passive income and does have offset restrictions. However, unless you are currently earning over $100,000 a year, don't worry yourself about it. When you make more than that, call me; I'll show you how to bypass the limits when you start owning bunches of income-producing properties.

4. Low Start-Up Costs

Sweat equity or trading in your old ski boat can easily make you the proud owner of an ugly, run-down duplex next to a garlic factory. Sure it stinks and it's not much to look at, but now you're a real estate investor. Here's what's really important. Your duplex will most likely increase in value as the rents go up. Ski boats, on the other hand, always go down in value; plus, they take up too much space in your garage. You need the extra space for your rental files anyway. This is an excellent trade if you pull it off.

The rental housing business can be quite inexpensive to start, if you don't get too picky about the looks. Uglier is better, but pay attention to location—no slums. Anywhere else is OK and, of course, don't overpay. (See my Income Property Analysis Form in Appendix B. Create one for yourself, fill it out, and you'll know exactly how much to pay for every property you buy.)

5. Forced Savings Plan

People who can't save money in a bank account can do it with investment houses. How? you ask. It's simple! With houses, you'll have your money invested while you fix them up. Chances are that you won't sell them very fast, and it's likely that by the time you could sell them, you'll have figured out that you probably shouldn't.

I know many folks in the real estate business who have gotten filthy rich, and it's not because they're overly smart. It's because once they're in, they can't get out quickly, so they just hang on. Hanging on, in case you don't know, is where the big money is. Once you pay off the mortgages, your houses are all yours without the debt. You keep all the money.

Free-and-clear houses are almost like owning your own personal bank. Although they're considered illiquid in one sense, houses are still great money generators. They produce monthly (cash flow) income. You can borrow on your equity and ultimately, of course, sell them for lots more money than you paid. If you save $10,000 at the bank's average passbook rate of 3.0 percent (it varies), you will earn $300 for one full year. If, instead, you invest $10,000 down on a $100,000 duplex that appreciates at the same passbook rate (3.0 percent), you've earned $3,000 during the same period of time. It doesn't take a rocket scientist to see which deal is better. The fact is, it's 10 times better and you'll end up rich a whole lot faster.

6. No Expensive Tools

When people ask me, "What is the most valuable tool you own?" my immediate response is "My toilet plunger." Obviously, plungers don't cost a great deal for the amount of action they stir up. Joking aside, there are no expensive start-up tools to buy. Any tools or equipment you may need can be acquired as you go along. Certainly a small pickup truck comes in handy, but that can be your next vehicle if you don't own one now. You won't be needing a fancy computer either. Maybe someday. But I can tell you this much from my own experience. Before you really need one, you'll have oodles of money to buy one. When it comes to making money, what you need most is a good sharp pencil and a yellow pad. That's it. Computers are fine for playing "what if" games. What you really need to know is how to buy fixer-upper houses. After years of buying houses and not owning a computer, I now have one for my publishing business. I paid cash for the whole setup out of my "toy" account.

7. Use of Leverage

No other business I know of allows your money to work so hard and accomplish so much; $10,000 can control a $100,000 duplex. That's a 10-to-1 leverage ratio. Using high leverage safely is the key to making big money in the rental housing business. It's very common to purchase income properties with 10-percent cash down payments. Fixer-upper houses can often be acquired for much less. The reason leverage helps you build wealth so fast is that you are able to control 100 percent of a property's moneymaking capability for only pennies on the dollar. For example, if I can purchase a $100,000 duplex for $10,000 cash down with rents of $1,000 per month, my cash return is $12,000 a year. There are very few legitimate opportunities available where $10,000 invested in anything will start returning $12,000 every year. It gets even better after a few rent increases. With the use of leverage and compounding, a mere $10,000 invested in duplexes, compounding annually at a rate of 50 percent, will grow to almost $600,000 in 10 short years.

8. Limited Personal Risk

When my friend with the fancy hot-air balloon machine signed the installment contract to purchase the setup, he became personally liable for all the payments. If he doesn't pay up, I'm sure, the franchise company won't want the hot-air machine back. The way the contract reads, it can take my friend's house, attach his wages, seize his bank account, and perhaps even take his firstborn.

In the rental housing business it's easy to avoid such a fate. With just a little know-how you can structure your notes and financial contracts to eliminate personal risk beyond the houses you purchase. It something goes haywire and you can't keep your promise to pay, you can simply give the houses back, but that's it. No more hassles, no midnight phone calls, and no personal risk. The secret here is to not sign any deals where you're responsible to give anything back except what you purchased to begin with. It's easy to do with fixer-upper houses.

9. No License Required

As a rule, owners don't need a license to work on property they own. The same goes for selling what they own. There are exceptions, but very few. A real estate license is required if you sell real estate for others or manage property for a fee. If you manage for an investor friend or partner, as I've done many times, my suggestion is to be very cautious. By receiving compensation other than fees, you will likely be all right. The general rule is, licenses are normally required if you hire yourself out to perform services for the public. If that's not what you're doing, chances are you'll be just fine.

Obviously, a good rule to follow is, don't advertise your personal business. Keep those matters to yourself. A final word of caution regarding permits. General repairs and painting don't normally get owners into much trouble. Fixing electrical and gas appliances is another story. Safety is involved. A licensed contractor takes you off the hook if something blows up. I strongly recommend to all who ask my opinion—don't do fix-up or repairs that involve a tenant's safety. Let the professionals do it, and you'll sleep much better.

10. Creating Long-Term Annuities

Certainly you've heard of life insurance annuities. You pay your premium for x number of years. Then one day, many years later, your premiums are paid in full. Your policy has now earned a cash value you can use. The rental housing business works exactly like that, only better. For one thing, it's much faster. Also, the ratio of the payback to what you contribute is far greater than any insurance policy I've ever seen. It has to do with the leverage and compounding we've already discussed. Also, there's the added safety of personal management. You have total control over your assets. For example, when real estate sales are at their peak (an up-cycle), you may decide to sell, taking full advantage of top-of-the-market prices (frenzy buying). The same thing applies with rent increases. The shortage of rental housing can produce much higher profits for owners who keep managing their rental properties year after year.

I like to look at my rental houses as long-term annuities. I buy them; I fix them up. After that, it's just a simple matter of keeping them maintained and rented. In return, they keep me supplied with fresh green money while my tenants pay them off. That's a fair trade, don't you think?

11. Rents Never Stop

You may have a good job with sick leave and other perks, but many people don't. That's where my rental houses shine. If I get sick and don't work, I still collect my rents like clockwork. Sure, I'm responsible for upkeep, but that doesn't mean I personally do the work. The truth is, I quit doing my own maintenance work years ago. My fix-up crew does it now.

Many business opportunities I'm familiar with don't produce any income when the owner is not performing. Take my friend with his hot-air machine. If he suddenly gets sick and stops snapping those pictures and blowing up balloons, he won't generate much income at the county fair next week. The bad news is, he still has those contract payments to make. Nonstop rental income allows a tremendous amount of flexibility for income property owners. It means you can arrange your personal schedule so it benefits you the most. Weekend activities can be done on Wednesdays. Vacations can be taken any time you feel like you need one. Here's the bottom line—once you get your houses set up, online, and earning rents, it's like a guaranteed income forever as long as you keep them maintained and filled with paying customers.

12. Automatic Retirement Nest Egg

One of the most rewarding financial benefits of all comes at the end. For many folks, retirement means cutbacks and reduction in the quality of their living standard. Typically, retirement plans provide about half the income people have become accustomed to living on. That's definitely not the kind of retirement income you must settle for if you own income-producing real estate.

My good friend, the late Bill Nickerson, spent most of his life in this business. For many years Bill operated a large apartment building in the San Francisco Bay area. His rents were $600,000 annually. The exciting part was that Bill had long since paid off his mortgage. I would guess Bill had a few bucks left over each month after expenses for his retirement years. Many folks take the easy way out. They sell their properties and take out well-secured notes that provide monthly income without the management responsibilities. With secured notes they are free to travel or do whatever they wish in their retirement years.

Perhaps you've noticed, I've never once mentioned age with respect to retirement. That's because there is no age requirement. Since you are the only person who will determine how fast you wish to invest, how many properties you'd like to own, and how much money will make you happy, it only follows you're the one who must also decide what age is right for you to retire. Like everything else about this business, the choice is always yours to make.

6

You Can't Hit a Bird with a Buffalo Gun:
Common Mistakes First-Timers Make

In this chapter you will learn about:

- How trying new ideas can hurt you
- The trap of beautiful, over-financed houses
- Being wary of properties with no equity
- The truth about multiple mortgages and promissory notes

One of the few advantages of getting older, aside from getting richer (hopefully), is that you can look back over a long stretch of time and see exactly what you should have done to start with. Hindsight is a marvelous educator. I only wish it had come sooner. In this chapter I'll share some of my early mistakes—those that kept me from making big money. And I'll also share other moneymaking tips and investment strategies I've learned along the way.

Jack-of-All-Trades, Master of None

Jack-of-all-trades, master of none. That was how I started investing. Tell me about a new idea, and I'll try it out. Looking back, my thinking was that if I try them all, the odds of my hitting a home run are a whole lot better. Investors who are game for anything that sounds like a good deal are much like hunters who don't know what they're hunting. Should you meet one in the woods and ask, "What are you hunting today?" their answer may be, "Don't know, I haven't seen anything yet!" Silly as that might sound, if you substitute "investor" for "hunter," it's quite obvious that this happens all the time. How in the world can you be a hunter when you don't even know what you're hunting? How would you pick out the right gun to take along? The answer is you can't. The same applies to investors who don't know what they're hunting. If your thinking is something like mine was, I've got bad news for you. You probably can't get there (rich) from here. You'll have far better results if you pick a specialty, learn it well, and repeat it often. Be the very best in your town doing it. That's where the big paydays come from. It's OK to branch out later on, but learn to do one thing very well before moving on to another.

Take my advice—develop a workable investment plan first, and then follow the plan. Hopefully someday when you look back, you'll see that you've avoided many serious mistakes. One other point—it's my guess you'll have the extra money to prove it.

Forget Sellers Who Can't Make You a Good Deal

In order to acquire properties at bargain prices or prices that will allow you to make a reasonable profit, you must first determine if the property can actually be purchased for a reasonable price. OK, I hear you thinking to yourself, "Boy, this don't seem so tough! Why can't I just ask the seller? Certainly he can tell me in a minute." Friends, here's a bit of advice. Sellers may not understand that they have problems, especially if they paid too much themselves.

Many times I've found very desirable properties for sale, but they're seriously over-financed. Owners (sellers) who have over-financed properties are often extremely eager to sell and for little or no cash down payments. The reason is to stop their negative cash flow. You must beware of these kind of properties. An over-financed property can spell big trouble, no matter how small the down payment is. Once you determine how much you can afford to pay for a property and still make money for yourself, you must drop the whole idea if it looks like the purchase price will exceed your estimate. Sellers with too much existing debt have very limited flexibility for negotiating the price downward. Conversely, sellers with lots of equity also have lots of room to reduce their asking prices. These are the sellers you're looking for.

Quite often you'll find sellers who have over-financed their real estate by paying too much in the first place or by adding loans during their ownership. The reason doesn't matter much. These sellers are simply not in a position to make you a very good deal. The only way they could would be to pay down the existing debt or to pay you money to take their property. Obviously, those are not attractive options for most sellers. The simple truth is that when too much money is already owed on the property, it can seldom be a good deal for you. Don't waste your time fiddling with deals that don't show you a clear plan for making reasonable profits.

Don't Fiddle with Sellers Who Have No Equity

Properties that have been owned by a seller for a substantial period of time, 6 to 10 years or more, will offer good opportunities for negotiating the selling price downward. The reason is that the existing mortgage debt has most likely been paid down over the years. It's always to your advantage to negotiate a purchase price when only the seller's equity is at stake.

For example, let's say the seller is asking $250,000. You can assume the existing mortgage of $195,000; the balance, or the seller's equity, is $55,000. Let's assume you've done your homework and concluded that $210,000 is the right price to pay. If the seller accepts, he or she will receive $15,000 for the equity. The seller most likely will not like it but is still getting something from the sale. Now consider the situation if the seller had purchased the property only a year earlier for a price of $235,000. The down payment was $20,000, so the seller still owes almost $215,000 on the mortgage. Your chances of buying this property for $210,000 just flew out the window. To do it, the seller would need to pay you $5,000 to buy the property. Even if it would help the seller financially, emotionally it's almost too much of an obstacle to overcome. In short, this seller is not in a position to make you a good deal.

An Opportunity You Shouldn't Pass Up: Taking Over Existing Mortgages

Many buyers are hesitant to purchase properties with multiple mortgages and promissory notes on them. I am exactly the opposite. The more notes I can assume or take over, the better I like the deal. In fact, I am constantly on the lookout for properties with multiple notes. Quite often I'm even willing to pay a bit more for them.

First, let me explain that private party notes or mortgages are the kind I'm looking for, not mortgages from banks or regular institutional lenders. My detective work involves finding out whom is owed the money on the notes (called the *beneficiaries*). I want to know if they are rich, poor, or out of work, whether they live out of the area, whether they are young or old, and whether they have children who might need money for college and, if so, how soon from now. People always ask me at seminars, "Why do you care about that stuff?" I'm trying to determine whether or not I'll be able to buy the note back at a discount price once I become the owner of the property. Beneficiaries who need cash or think they do are the ones who will sell for big discounts.

For example, let's say I purchase a property and assume or take over a private note with a balance of $45,000 with monthly payments of $435. The note was originally a 20-year term, and it still has 14 years of payments left. Mrs. Smith, a 36-year-old divorcee, holds the note. She received it in her divorce settlement. Her only son, Johnny, is now 15 years old and a junior in high school. He has his heart set on attending college in a couple of years. As I see it, there's an excellent chance I'll be providing for Johnny's higher education when I make an offer to purchase the note for $26,000 cash two years from now. That's a savings of almost $9,000. If that doesn't make you take a second look at taking over notes, I don't know what will.

7

Planning Your Profits at the Kitchen Table

In this chapter you will learn about:

- Advantages to being your own boss
- Property sales: alternatives to large cash payments
- Creative loans that work in your favor
- Getting paid when you buy a property

When I first started buying houses in Redding, California, counting my real estate profits was easy. I remember sorting out the rent money I would gather in from my four little Pine Street houses. The accounting was easy; I collected rents from my tenants, put it in the bank, and then wrote out a check for almost the same amount to make my monthly mortgage payment.

Over the years, the amount of money I took in changed considerably. Obviously 200 houses take more accounting effort than those first four rentals. However, one thing has always stayed the same—I still operate my housing business from the same kitchen table I started on. Naturally, I've had to add the center leaf to create more room for stacking money, and I've moved the table several times to bigger houses. My point is that housing entrepreneurship is the best home-operated business opportunity I know of. I will gladly match my income with that of any other so-called stay-at-home work-for-yourself business. Real estate, the way I do it, beats 'em all!

The Advantage of Being Your Own Boss

To begin with, I talk to the boss every morning in the shower. Not surprisingly, we are in perfect agreement with my plans for the day. No changes or compromises are ever necessary unless I say OK. Being your own boss is undoubtedly the most sought-after dream of every W-2 working stiff. No time clocks, no lay-offs, and no more commuter rush. Most folks, given a choice, would drastically change their personal lifestyles if earning a living at their jobs were not the most important priority. Obviously eating is a tough habit to break. Therefore, working for money is necessary. But, there are many ways to earn money besides working for someone else. We'll explore my method as we go along, but first take a good look at several of the benefits of self-employment.

Let me start out this way—when I get up in the morning, there's no rush to chase down the freeway or make an excuse for being late. My mornings are leisurely. I can plan my day. Sometimes my plan changes, but for the most part I'm in total control. I like being in control of my life. I enjoy being in a position to do what I want when I want. That's not an option for most people who work at 9-to-5 jobs. I know because I did that for over 20 years.

Daily Running Is on My Schedule

I love to jog two or three miles every day. Some say jogging is harder than working at a regular job. If you don't like exercise, I suppose that's true. But I enjoy jogging, so I do it. My point here is that I can allow myself the time to do it, when I want to. The way my schedule works, I normally run in the late mornings, like 10:30 or 11 A.M. The trail along the river is always a bit cooler than anywhere else in town. People are always asking me why I don't run early like other joggers. The reason is because I like to do my writing and real estate planning, such as penciling out deals, first thing in the morning. Obviously, I don't want my running to interfere with those activities, but I can still do the things I wish to do when I choose to do them.

Years ago, when I worked for the telephone company, trips and vacations had to be scheduled well in advance. They had to fit the available time when my workload wasn't heavy. I like to take trips, even if they're short ones, without waiting for weekends or work to taper off. My kitchen table job—working for myself—allows me to do that. It's one of the many personal benefits of being the boss and chairman of the board.

No Pink Slip from Yourself

Today I'm fireproof. I'll never need to worry about a layoff notice or getting fired ever again. Those things happen to employees, and they happen all too often today, as anyone can see by reading the local newspaper.

Obviously self-employment would be quite similar to getting laid off if your earnings weren't sufficient. If you follow my kitchen table investment strategies, hopefully you can avoid such a fate. I would never suggest you give up any source of income until you find a better source. Becoming a real estate entrepreneur is without question a better source if you can make it happen.

Three Ways to Bring Home Dollars

Kitchen table operators don't get W-2s every year to show bank loan officers. Anyone who has ever tried to borrow money from a bank knows full well that no W-2 usually translates into no loan. Furthermore, generally loan officers don't like self-employed folks too much to begin with. Since the officers must work 9 to 5 (show up), they reason, why shouldn't everyone have to? Also, most self-employed real estate investors generally do a lousy job of explaining to bankers how they intend to pay the loan back. As a result, most bankers rely on that overworked expression, "just say no."

Don't get the idea that borrowing is out. It's not. However, I can assure you that it's a lot more difficult for self-employed types. Therefore, new full-time investors should never bet the ranch on the hopes of borrowing money from conventional lenders. Basically I get money (green stuff) from three primary sources.

They are:

1. Rental income (monthly cash flow)
2. Property sales
   A. Lump-sum cash through down payments at closing
   B. Monthly payments through carryback notes
3. Borrowing
   A. Lump-sum cash through owner subordination to new loans at purchase
   B. Lump-sum cash through conventional loans and hard money mortgages

We discuss each of these methods in more detail later. First, let me tell you how important it is to have all three sources available as options at all times. You need to realize there are times when it seems like you can't give real estate away. You try to sell. You lower the price. Still no offers. Oh sure, someone might offer to buy for 50 cents on the dollar, but that's no good. Besides, aren't you in this business to make money? Why would you give all the profits away? On the other hand, there are times (*up-cycles*, we call them) when buyers will pay almost any price. It's like a supermarket sale, 8 cents apiece, or three for a quarter. When people feel good about buying real estate, price doesn't matter too much. Obviously, that's the proper time for selling.

Steady Cash Flow Pays the Bills

Most important to real estate wealth building is the steady flow of cash. Steady flow means money coming in monthly you can depend on to pay the bills. Cash flow is often overlooked by novice investors seeking fame and fortune. To borrow words from the famous hamburger millionaire, Ray Kroc, founder of McDonald's, "It's most important to stay green and growing." Staying green means having enough income to pay the bills. This allows you to keep growing.

That's the one problem I have with investors who speculate. Speculators are all too often willing to tolerate short-term difficulties (lack of cash flow) in the hopes that they'll hit a super payday. More often than not, that payday never comes. After you've gone broke, it's too late. For this reason, I strongly recommend owning and operating rental units. By doing so, you'll always have cash flow generators to pay the bills. Also, I strongly suggest that rental units be the first investment. It's very important to build up your cash flow as quickly as possible. That should be your Number 1 order of business if you intend to stay in business for the long haul.

Selling Cycles: Catching the Perfect Wave

Giving away profits is not good business. This happens mostly when lack of cash flow makes it necessary for investors to sell their fixed-up properties quickly and at the wrong time. As I mention in Chapter 4, timing is a very important part of making big money. Surfers seek to catch the perfect wave. Real estate investors also seek to catch the perfect wave … by selling during an up-cycle. Ideally, we'd like to sell when scads of people are interested in buying properties. Up-cycles automatically drive up selling prices. This happens because lots of buyers are chasing after too few properties. It's a time when your property can be sold for the highest price and most favorable terms for you, the seller. When you have an adequate amount of cash flow from rentals, you're in the perfect position to wait for the proper timing (up-cycles) to make your sales. That's worth big bucks even though it means you must learn to be a landlord while you wait. Being a landlord and managing property will take a while to learn, but the benefits are well worth your efforts.

In my judgment, it's the complete real estate investor (entrepreneur) who stands the best chance of becoming the new millionaire on the block. Complete investors know when to hold 'em and when to fold 'em as Kenny Rogers sings in his song, "The Gambler." Never forget this part—selling for the highest price won't happen because you're ready to sell. It will happen when buyers are ready to buy. Therefore, I would strongly suggest that you time your selling for the right cycle. In the meantime, stay alive with the income from your cash flow rentals.

Property Sales: Lump-Sum Cash vs. Monthly Payments

There are many ways to become very wealthy without requiring large cash payments. It's a well-known fact that cash sales done without proper tax consideration or a workable plan to keep the dollars invested can often result in loss of capital. Loss of capital for any investor, especially in the early stages, will cause a serious growth problem. You could even say it's like going backwards.

I have sold many properties for thousands of dollars more than the average prevailing prices because I've provided excellent terms to buyers. When you consider all those extra dollars earning two or three times more interest than most banks earn from their loans, it's easy to see that carryback paper isn't all that bad for your financial health. Since notes and mortgages don't appreciate or grow in value, it's not wise to have all your assets in paper. A good balanced diet of note (mortgage) payments coming in, plus cash flow rental houses, makes for excellent investor nutrition.

All Borrowing Is Not the Same

Having good credit and the ability to borrow money from the bank won't necessarily make you a wealthy investor any more quickly than a person who can't borrow a dime. What it might do is make your buying properties a bit easier. Basically, what separates successful investors from those who are not is learning and using profit-making skills.

For example, I borrow money like most other investors. However, I don't waste my time trying to convince 30-year-old bank loan officers to fork over the bank's money on 60-year-old ugly houses. If somehow I got a loan, they'd probably fire the manager who approved the deal. The plain fact is, no matter how good I am at turning ugly ducklings into beautiful swans, I'm sure you can understand it's not the kind of risk most banks are looking for. Traditional bankers don't like ugly houses filled with deadbeat tenants. Instead, they'd rather loan money to some inexperienced idiot to build windmills on a hill without any wind, so long as it's government-guaranteed, as in SBA (Small Business Administration). Banks lust and crave guarantees. They don't like real estate borrowers with a big vision who are offering junky houses for security. That's simply the way it is, so we investors must adjust our borrowing needs to work around bank policies when we borrow from banks.

High-Risk Lenders Are Often the Only Source for Fix-Up Investors

Thrift lenders and individuals with money to loan are often the best (and only) source of loans available to new investors. It's true, the interest rates are higher, but for many investors, especially self-employed kitchen table operators like me when I started, it's the only game in town. The good news is that you probably won't need to fill out all those stupid bank forms, profit and loss statements, verification of income and employment, plus a truckload of worthless "rear-end protection" documents required by regular bankers. Normally these type of loans are straight equity loans without any personal liability. Obviously, that part is good. The bad part is that most lenders won't loan much more than 60 percent of the total property value. For example, you might get a $60,000 loan on a $100,000 property. Obviously an appraisal would be required in most cases.

Creative Loans from "Godfather Lenders"

By skillfully borrowing from a high-cost lender, it's still possible to get the job done and not pay much more interest in the long run. Here's an actual example of a loan I arranged for one of my properties a few years ago. To start with, the seller and I both agreed that the property needed work. The way the property looked, the owner was convinced that selling would be a difficult chore. At best, he could expect to receive no more than 10-percent cash down from any buyer. That would only be $15,000 based on his $150,000 asking price. He needed more cash than that. The property had an existing mortgage (loan) balance of $44,000, in amortized payments of $360 per month. I figure his equity was somewhere near $100,000. The seller's main motivation was getting more cash up front. This was the offer he accepted: $135,000 full price with $35,000 cash down payment. My offer was on the condition that the seller would subordinate his equity carryback note to a new "hard money" loan secured by the property in the amount of $45,000 ($35,000 to the seller and $10,000 to the buyer—me). I would use my $10,000 for fix-up on the property. That meant that the seller would carry back a note (owner financing) for $56,000. I also needed another favor. The monthly payment on the equity note ($56,000) would need to fit within the rental income limitations of the property. The seller agreed to 5-percent interest-only payments for the first 15 years ($233.33 per month), then 10-percent interest-only for 5 years ($466.66 per month), after which time (20 years) the entire loan balance would be due and payable.

How to Get Paid When You Buy the Property

In this particular transaction, the property was at least 45 years old, but it looked 100. No bank loan officer of sound mind would have touched it with a 10-foot pole. Still, I was able to borrow real green money from a thrift lender (Beneficial Finance–type) based solely on the property equity and a subordination agreement from the seller. This deal actually put $10,000 in my pocket, less my share of escrow expenses at the closing.

People often ask me, "How do you ever find sellers who will go along with this type of transaction?" The answer is really quite simple. You find sellers who are motivated and have a real need to sell. Often their properties are extremely difficult to sell. In this particular transaction, the property was very unsightly (like a pigsty) and very run down—no one who looked it over wanted to buy it in such terrible condition. I was the only one who made an offer the seller could accept. Even though my equity loan was at 16 percent interest, it was amortized for 15 years. When you blend it with the low-interest seller financing I received, you can see that the net results to me were a reasonable cost of financing the deal. After all, I paid nothing down and received $10,000 of the loan money myself, plus I'm the proud owner of an income-producing property. I think you might agree with me—this method is not a bad way to borrow money.

Trading Soggy Paper for Hard Dollars

Another borrowing technique I've used with excellent results combines trading my carryback notes (mortgages) for down payments, and then borrowing hard money against my newly acquired property. What this accomplishes is trading my weak or soggy paper for income property at full face value. I have never had to discount my notes when I use them for down payments.

Soggy paper is a term used to express less desirable notes, usually seller carryback notes from an ugly property sale. Often they are long-term mortgages with low interest rates and contain no restrictive conditions, such as a due-on-sale clause, prepay penalty, or even late fee charges. They have a very low cash value for the purpose of selling them outright. The major benefit to this technique is that it avoids discounting the note as one might normally expect when selling the note for cash. Obviously in the transaction above, my success is largely dependent on finding exactly the right seller. Naturally that's my biggest job, but it's worth all the effort.

Buying property with a note or mortgage works like this. First, you must find sellers who don't want their property anymore. Perhaps the tenants plan to hang them next time they show their faces on the property. These kinds of owners are very likely to jump at your offer to take your note as the down payment. Often, the note by itself is enough, but sometimes it may take a little cash "sweetener" tossed in for good measure. This is called a *lemonade offer*. The cash part is the sugar; the note (paper) would be the lemons.

For example, let's say the seller has a $200,000 property she wants out of. She tells me there's a $40,000 mortgage balance, which I can assume. So far, so good. Here's what I'll do using this technique. I offer $200,000, full price. My down payment will be the assignment of a $120,000 note I currently own with monthly payments (income) of $1,000. I will then ask the seller to carry back a new note or mortgage in the amount of $40,000 for the balance of her equity. That's it! If the seller agrees, I'm the owner of a $200,000 property. But equally important, I'm in a position to borrow hard money if I need to. I have created $120,000 equity.

Assuming the property is worth $200,000 or is appraised for that, most lenders would allow me to borrow at least 60 percent of LTV (loan-to-value). If the property is dirty or has vacancies when I close escrow, I always arrange for some cleanup before applying for a loan. Remember, most everyone on the planet, which includes lenders, passes judgment based on looks. You'll have much better success borrowing if your property looks good. In this example, we have $80,000 total debt on a $200,000 property. I can reasonably expect to (pull out) borrow $40,000 on a straight equity loan. Assuming all this works out, here's what I've accomplished on the deal.

First, I've traded a $120,000 depreciating asset (the note) at full face value (no discount) for a $200,000 appreciating asset (the property). I've also pocketed $40,000 cash on the deal. This is the way to borrow most effectively, in my judgment, because you get a lot more value for your money. There's even more value than first meets the eye. Do you recall those selling cycles we talked about earlier? That's when my $120,000 note originated. Back then when buyers were standing in line to buy my property, I was able to sell it for $50,000 more than I anticipated. Naturally, I gave good terms to the buyer. Anyway, that's how I ended up with a $120,000 equity note. Had I not timed my sale to the proper cycle, my note could have easily been for $70,000 instead. As I said earlier, timing is an important part of making big money.

Paying enormous fees or points to borrow money makes very little sense to me. The same goes for selling notes at steep discounts in order to generate "walking around" money. Pulling out cash when you purchase a property or from properly timed selling should provide you with enough everyday cash to buy a large kitchen table for counting your blessings. Meantime, take my advice about rental properties seriously. Rent money will keep the wolves away until you've had time to learn how to rake in the serious money. It takes a little time to learn all this stuff, but you're going to be a very happy camper when you see the results.

PART 2

Buying Your First Investment Houses

8

Properties with All the Right Things Wrong

In this chapter you will learn about:

- Getting started
- Properties that can be purchased with no money down
- Owners who provide the best terms
- How underperforming properties are top moneymakers

People constantly ask me, "What kind of investing do you recommend for ordinary working folks with only a few dollars to invest and a limited amount of time?" I have no trouble whatsoever answering because, in my opinion, one answer fits both for most working folks. My one-size-fits-all recommendation is to invest your money and your time in income-producing residential properties. That's it!

Getting Started

Beyond desire and willingness to become a successful investor, getting started ranks at the top of the list. Starting is without question the one important difference between investors who become financially independent and the rest who merely wish they were. Many folks have high hopes and the best intentions, but they always seem to be waiting for something to happen. Whatever they think is supposed to happen rarely does. Waiting to have enough money to start investing is probably the most overworked excuse for doing nothing. It's also one of the lamest that I know, because many successful investors start with hardly anything but desire.

Let's assume you wish to acquire income- or profit-producing real estate with very little money. You can contribute time and labor. In other words, you are raring to go right now. First, I want you to ask yourself two questions. The answers are intended to guide you as well as to maximize your personal efforts. This idea might seem a little strange at first. However, once you find a good deal, strange ideas will begin to seem a lot more natural to you, I promise, so bear with me and I'll explain.

What Kind of Property Might You Expect to Purchase Without a Cash Down Payment?

Here are a couple of suggestions to help you decide:

1. Run-down houses with the kinds of tenants who scare most people.
2. Tenant problems (motorcycles, junk autos, and pigsty houses).
3. Empty property, tall weeds, broken glass, garbage everywhere.
4. Financial problems (foreclosures, bankruptcy, bank repossession).

5. Partially completed building (all activity stopped), as in "went broke."

The reason you are looking for distressed properties and problem tenants is that they represent big problems for the owners. The idea is to use your time and personal efforts to fix these problems in lieu of making the regular cash down payments. Correcting problems has cash value.

Often the price to correct big problems will amount to a much higher dollar value than the normal amount of a cash down payment. The point is that your ambition and ability to fix problems for others can create an excellent opportunity for you. Few investors are willing to try, so you'll stand out.

Many investors, including me, have used this wealth-building technique to quickly develop large real estate portfolios. It's a perfect solution for someone without down-payment cash, which of course is almost everyone who subscribes to my wealth-building techniques.

What Kinds of Sellers Are Likely to Own the Types of Property Described?

Here are some likely candidates:

1. Out-of-town owners who are not paying attention to what goes on at their rental properties.
2. Owners with health or financial problems.
3. Owners with family problems: divorce, death, and destitution (the three Ds).
4. Owners who place for-sale-by-owner ads (all newspapers).
5. Owners who have lost their jobs and can't pay their bills.
6. Those who want to retire or are elderly or disabled.
7. Owners who have inherited property—easy-come, easy-go mentality.

8. Owners who advertise lease-option or house for rent.
9. Owners who had to move for work reasons and now have two house payments.

An important point to remember is that people won't always tell you what their true motivation is. Owners who advertise a property seeking a lease-option could easily be searching for a way to rid themselves of managing a property they can't sell. Most out-of-town owners don't like long-distance renting, especially with problem tenants, but they seldom tell you that's the reason. You must learn to operate like a detective and find the answers for yourself.

Inheritance owners often think rental houses are too much hassle. After all, they weren't the ones who bought the stupid property in the first place. Owners with financial problems or those with two mortgage payments will seldom tell you they're hurting when in fact they really are. You must learn to dig out this kind of information in order to prepare an offer that will create a high level of interest for the seller.

Leper Properties Make the Most Money

Sellers are motivated, no down payments are acceptable, and, best of all, run-down "leper" properties are the biggest money-makers. Leper properties that have worked best for me have been the older multi-units, often add-on types where additional units have been built on the property over the years. They are found in the older residential neighborhoods and also in commercially zoned areas in the older sections of most cities. This is where folks lived before freeways and sprawling suburban subdivisions.

These kinds of properties often started out as a single-family house on a large city lot. Over the years, units were added—

granny apartments, they're often called. You might find a duplex or several cottages in the rear yard behind the main house or perhaps efficiency apartments above the garage. Zoning wasn't a big issue years ago, and many owners built backyard rental units to supplement their retirement incomes. Today you'll discover many of these units in run-down condition after years of neglect. I call them *leper properties*. Few investors want to touch them.

Leper properties can be acquired for a much lower unit price than regular apartment-type properties. Single house buyers don't want them; apartment buyers don't want them either. Real estate agents don't know whether to sell them to investors or homeowners. Consequently, they tend to fall through the cracks from a marketing standpoint. Here are several important points to remember:

1. There's much less competition to acquire leper properties.
2. Tenants (renters) like this kind of property—more privacy and mature landscaping.
3. Rents are equivalent to newer units of comparable size, yet the purchase price per unit is much lower.
4. Ideal for do-it-yourself house fixers because top skills are not required. Any work you do will most likely make the property look better.
5. Seller financing is often the only financing available because zoning is wrong for residential units. Banks don't like that. But remember, the use of property as residential units is grandfathered as long as the units remain residential.
6. Because of unit cost, easy-term seller financing, and being the popular choice among tenants, leper properties can achieve cash flow status faster than any other type of rentals I know of.

Underperforming Properties Are Best Value

Leper properties or junk houses that rent for $300 in a $400 rent market are a perfect example of what I mean by adding value. To start with, I would likely pay out 5 times the gross rents for units renting at 30 percent below market value. Let's say we have 8 units at $300 rents. That's $2,400 per month or $28,800 annually. Purchase price equals 5 times $28,800 ($144,000).

The value of a property that commands top market rents of $400 per unit doesn't stay valued at 5 times gross rents the way it does when it's run down and under-rented at $300 per unit per month. Instead, it's quite likely to be valued around 7 times gross rents after the property is fixed up and looks attractive. You can see there's a big difference: 8 units at $400 rents equals $3,200 per month or $38,400 annually. Seven times $38,400 comes to a new value of $268,800. If you have the ability to discover what's wrong and fix it, you could earn $124,800 for your efforts. Suppose it takes you a year or two. It still beats welding fenders down at the Ford plant.

Keep a Clear View of the Big Picture

The strategy I've suggested here works very well. It's not some Disneyland scheme that only works once in your lifetime. Obviously, there are as many different variations to this technique as your imagination will allow. Once you start making telephone calls and begin talking with potential sellers, you'll be pleasantly surprised to find out how creative you can be. For example, I've conducted transactions in which my full down payment was a ski boat or an old pickup truck. There are many ways to acquire real estate besides using hard cash when you put your thinking cap on.

People problems and the run-down condition of properties are the most common factors that determine how weak or how strong your offer needs to be. As you gain experience doing a few deals, you'll look back from time to time, as I do, wondering if you didn't give too much away. Don't harbor thoughts like this for long, because even if you did, so what? You'll end up filthy rich just the same. In the overall scheme of things, paying a few thousand dollars extra will hardly hurt you at all. What will hurt you is not going after these deals in the first place.

Some years ago I acquired a seven-unit property filled with threatening-looking bikers for about half the price it would have sold for without them. The owner was so afraid of his tenants that he wouldn't even show me the property. He told me he wasn't going near the place. After a quick drive-by, I simply filed eviction papers with the court, and the marshal served my papers. Not long afterwards, the bikers were seen rolling down the interstate about an hour ahead of the scheduled toss-out time. All I had to do was clean up a big mess to earn $126,000 in just seven months. It will pay you to start looking at the kind of income-producing properties you're reading about. The rewards are well worth your efforts.

9

Property Selection Determines Your Profits

> ## In this chapter you will learn about:
>
> - Knowing your customer before you buy
> - The Hillcrest Cottages: How solving problems pays well
> - Five house conditions for unbeatable discounts and buying terms
> - The yellow-pad method: Estimating your income and profits *before* you buy

If you purchase real estate without first preparing a reasonable plan for what you're going to do with it, you could easily end up in big trouble and not even realize it. My telephone mentor service has taught me dozens of different ways investors can mess themselves up—more ways than I ever imagined existed. Talking on the telephone with customers has provided me with a long list of things investors shouldn't do to themselves.

I get calls from investors almost daily asking me if it's a good deal for them to purchase a house for 30 percent under the appraisal value. Obviously, there's no way I could know the answer. I generally ask them what the purchase price is. They tell me $95,000. Next I ask how much they can rent the place for. They say $750, they think. I then ask how much comparable houses in the neighborhood rent for. They don't know, but somewhere between $700 and $800 seems about right, they say. "Are there lots of $750 renters?" I ask. "Don't know," they say. It's just about at this point that I tell them they're not quite ready to do any business yet. You've got to get yourself prepared before you stick your neck in a noose and can't pull it back out. Mark Twain once said that it took him two weeks to prepare for an impromptu speech. I wouldn't think buying houses and trying to make a profit would take anything less. Unprepared real estate investors are a lot like sheep headed for the slaughterhouse. Perhaps a few can succeed on pure luck, but the odds are very heavily stacked against them.

Know Who Your Customer Will Be Before You Buy

In the case of the $95,000 house, which is appraised for $136,000 or so, maybe it's a good deal and maybe it's not. Without more information, I can't really know. For example, if all the other houses around it are selling for $100,000 or so, then what good is a 30-percent-below-appraisal price? That's no bargain. If you live in a low-income area, like I do, where less than 10 percent of the total renting population can pay $700 or more per month, you must ask yourself: Will there be enough customers (renters) to keep the house rented? You certainly don't need a bunch of $750 rental houses without a matching supply of $750 renters. Buying at 30 percent under appraisal could still sink your ship if you buy before you know the answer.

Smart People Often Do the Stupidest Things

I shall always be amazed at the number of intelligent-looking folks who seem to think real estate investing is nothing more than buying three-bedroom houses with 10-percent down on the advice of someone passing through town making a pitch. Assuming someone does this with the $95,000 house in our discussion here, let's take a look at how things might turn out. If this someone is lucky enough to buy in with a 10 percent down payment for a nonowner-occupied property, then there's the matter of financing the other 90 percent. Fixed-rate mortgages for rental houses will always cost you more than your personal residence when it comes to long-term financing. Many lenders have nothing to offer except variable-interest-rate mortgages period, but let's just pretend we can find a fixed-rate, 30-year mortgage at 9 percent for a rental house. Principal and interest will add up to a monthly payment of $684.

That's just the finance cost, and, as you might guess, we're not quite done with expenses yet. No matter how tightly we manage, and of course we're doing it for free, there's still property taxes, insurance, maintenance such as painting, repairs when something breaks, and some occasional downtime when a tenant moves out. No matter how you slice it—or ignore it—total expenses will still cost 30–35 cents out of every rent dollar that comes in. Right off the bat we have a glaring problem here. That $684 mortgage payment gobbles up about 90 percent of the $750 income. Adding 90 percent to 30 percent should give you a pretty fair idea that something's not right. In this example, we would need another $160 every month just to break even while we're managing the house for nothing.

If you're faced with a proposition that resembles anything like the one we're discussing here, I suggest you step back and take a good hard look before you sign anything. If you're $160 negative, or upside down as they say in the used-car business, don't try to solve the problem with volume. If my message is too late, just don't do it again because you should be smarter now. To begin with, if you're like 99 percent of the investors I communicate with, chances are you paid $10,000 cash down, and, because the mortgage payment is slightly less than the monthly rent, you've told yourself it's a good deal. Hopefully, I've convinced you to take a harder look. You need to explain how you will benefit from an investment property with an $85,000 institutional mortgage and a deficit of $160 or more every month. Believe me, this is not some far-fetched uncommon example. On the contrary, it's very typical of the deals I'm hearing about. To me it doesn't sound like a very good plan for making money. OK, so what's wrong, you ask?

For starters, you certainly can't sell for a profit anytime soon. Adding value seems out of the question. After all, a $95,000 house in a $100,000 neighborhood tells me that you're already up to the value limits. You can't borrow money, so refinancing is out, and there's a real good chance the mortgage contains a due-on-sale provision, which could legally block you from selling on a wraparound (a small profit opportunity). A due-on-sale clause can also prevent you from doing a lease-option contract to improve the cash flow. If you're starting to see the big picture here, that's good. The only salvation the owner has in this example is appreciation, which of course, no one can predict.

Seminars Provide an Opportunity to Learn

Students who attend Fixer Camps in Redding, California, are taught many different ways to profit from investment properties. Cash flow investing has always been my Number 1 specialty, and how to do it is taught the first day of camp. When you understand what benefits are most important, you'll be able to zero in on the kinds of properties that provide them. You'll quickly learn that 80 percent or more of the available houses simply don't provide potential for profit-making anytime in the foreseeable future. Houses like the one we've been discussing here are dead-end deals because they tie you down to a single option, playing the appreciation game. That's like having one good artery to your heart. I teach students how to acquire properties that provide multiple benefits and maximum investor control. That strategy puts you in a position to profit many ways.

You'll learn why I purchase run-down houses where many opportunities or profit centers are available with the same property. Forced appreciation, EZ-term seller financing, no due-on-sale clauses, selling with wraparound notes, buying back debt, and lease options are all possible on my deals.

My Hillcrest Cottages: How Solving Problems Pays Well

I have always believed that in order to make things happen financially, you must make yourself ready for when the right deal comes knocking. Many start-out investors are standing on a gold mine, but they can't visualize it. You must prepare yourself for opportunity. Every licensed real estate agent in my town drove out to look at the Hillcrest Cottages at least once. They usually drove out before lunch because the deadbeat occupants were not up and about yet. If their clients observed the tenants congregating at the pool on a hot Redding afternoon, they would have switched real estate agents in a heartbeat. Most would-be buyers, but especially new investors, are not mentally prepared to witness such a mess, much less analyze its profit potential. To this day, I'm almost certain I was the only serious buyer who ever set foot on the Hillcrest property. My dream of fixing up the property would eventually turn out to be very profitable for me.

Hillcrest had everything wrong with it you could imagine. Not just the physical "board and brick" run-down condition that was clearly visible, but also foreclosure was knocking at the door. The city building department was already loading up its bulldozer in case the owners (two fighting partners) did not immediately start fixing numerous code violations. The old well (water supply) with broken sewer pipes nearby had local health authorities up in arms. The local police drove out two or three times per evening, attempting to encourage unruly occupants and their guests to act like decent folk and take less medication.

The Big Reward: Seller Concessions

At my seminars I continually advise my students that your bank account will grow much faster and become a whole lot fatter if you can look beyond the ugliness of the mine shaft and see the glitter of gold inside. With most run-down properties, ugliness is shallow but it's what shows. Naturally, what shows creates the undesirable image. After a little experience, most house fixers agree, ugliness like beauty is only skin deep and is quickly erased with a whole lot less effort than one might imagine.

The big reward for house fixers who learn how to solve ugly-house problems is seller concessions. Sellers who have problems are highly motivated to make deals. It's these deals that earn big money. I continually watch investors trying to purchase real estate from sellers who have little motivation to sell. There is simply no way to make a cash flow deal with folks who might sell with enough persuasion. Obviously, terms like seller financing and discount prices don't come from sellers who are still proud of what they're selling. For every barn-burner transaction I've ever made, there has always been a seller who has very few options to bargain with.

No Money Down Comes from Seller Motivation

My no-money-down offer for the Hillcrest property was quite readily accepted because no one else was competing. I agreed to pay the asking price, which I considered reasonable, so long as the sellers accepted my house trade for the down payment. As is the case with many trades, there's plenty of room for creativity. The sellers had already agreed on what their equity was worth, so just as quick as I heard the dollar number, I created my house price to match their number. Let me emphasize, there's no way you can make these deals fly without serious seller motivation. So with no cash down payment, I simply took over (assumed) three mortgages on the property and became the proud new owner of Hillcrest.

I would never advise new investors to begin their house-fixing career with a property with all the problems of Hillcrest. However, it would certainly make an excellent third or fourth project after the investor has served an apprenticeship working on smaller properties. Naturally, we all must walk before we can run, but when the time arrives that you're comfortable with a bigger challenge, don't forget that problem solving pays more money than any other activity in the real estate business. The sellers at Hillcrest were constantly fighting and arguing with their tenants. This is hardly the way to build good customer relations with the folks you're counting on to pay all your expenses.

Understanding Where Discounts Come From

Numbers always tell the story best, so allow me to explain about fixing up houses for big money. First, lots of people can fix up houses just fine, but the big majority of them come up pitifully short with the money part. They simply don't earn much money for all their time and effort. You must first understand that people get paid for their skills. You won't make a killing in the fix-up business from painting a house or hanging shutters. The house will certainly look a little better, but your bank statement won't.

Following is my list of five conditions that create the largest purchase discounts and most liberal buying terms. Ultimately these conditions will create the biggest paydays for fixer-upper investors.

Condition	Discount Range
1. Ugliness: looks like a pigsty, tons of junk	30–50 percent
2. People problems: unruly, dead-beats, non-paying	30–40 percent
3. Older houses: junk, deferred maintenance	25–35 percent
4. Run-down houses: out-of-town owners, tenant managers	20–30 percent
5. Cosmetic fixer-upper: needs paint, minor tuneup	10–15 percent

These conditions are based on my personal experiences after doing fix-up for many years. Hopefully, they will give you a good idea where the most money can be made in the fix-up business. Also, keep in mind that these five conditions are quite often found in combinations. Property ugliness combined with people problems are an almost unbeatable combination when it comes to profit-making. The bigger the problems you learn to solve, the larger the profits you'll earn.

Positioning Counts for Everything

You can't make any serious money if you are not in the right situation to do what needs to be done. Owning real estate can work you to death. It can put wrinkles on your face long before they're due naturally and even destroy you financially if you buy the wrong properties or pay too much. Investing has far too much risk and wear and tear if you don't make money in the process. The good news, however, is that you can make money, but you must plan for it and position yourself to accomplish the task.

Suppose you purchase the $95,000 house. Let's assume it rents for $750 per month and there are plenty of renters available. My question to you is "What now?" If one of the benefits you are seeking from investment property is making lots of money, could you please cut me in on your plans for doing it? Somehow I have a feeling the thrill of ownership is going to vanish before too long.

A Method for Extracting the Profits

Many investors buy houses without the slightest idea of how they'll make a profit. Others buy real estate and more or less figure that when it's time to sell, profits will automatically be there for them. Investing in this fashion is an easy path to failure. It involves too much speculation or guessing rather than investing.

When you have limited funds, like 95 percent of all my subscribers, you must make a thorough analysis or projection of future profits before you close escrow on every purchase. You need to understand exactly how each investment will pay you back when you own it. One method is to explain it thoroughly to an unsympathetic spouse who would rather use the down payment for a trip to Disneyland. If you can pass this test, chances are you've already given considerable thought to the deal, which is exactly my point here.

Pencils and Yellow-Pad Accounting

My method is a very simple one, which has served me well for a good many years. My tools consist of a yellow legal pad and a couple of pencils. I sketch out a sort of credit-debit schematic of a cash flow chart showing all the dollars I expect to spend in each year of my ownership. I also estimate my income or profits for every year. These income figures represent all the monies I expect the property to pay me during my period of ownership. Last, I estimate my future selling price and develop a realistic plan for making the sale. By going through this exercise, I'm forced to take a hard look at the various factors that contribute to a profitable investment, and, of course, that's the main purpose of the exercise. Take it from me, if you can't show someone on paper how you intend to make your profits, chances are you won't make any.

10

The Soap Factory Houses: A Virtual Gold Mine

In this chapter you will learn about:

- How realtors can miss the diamond in the rough
- Rental houses that act as moneymaking machines
- How high rent-to-value ratios equal gold
- When appreciation doesn't matter

Not long ago, a young man came to me with a problem. He had an opportunity to buy six dumpy houses extremely cheaply. Just about the time he was set to close the deal, a local real estate agent advised him that he would lose his shirt. The reason the agent gave was the location. The houses were located directly behind a soap factory. They would never appreciate in value, plus there was a better than average chance that he'd be stuck with them forever.

That's typical salesperson advice, and it' agent could be absolutely right. The problem ers on. He's already thinking about future sa tion. Those things just might not be too impc ation. In fact, as you will see, they're really ...., ..., including real estate professionals, are quite good when it comes to finding shiny gold nuggets that sparkle brightly in open view. However, their detection abilities diminish quite rapidly when the golden nuggets are slightly dusty or buried beneath the mud.

Remember this well—gold mines are not valuable because of their location or how they look. Most of them are smelly caves or holes in the ground, and most are rather ugly. The point I'm making here is that the value is not always apparent on the surface.

High Rent-to-Value Ratio Produces Gold

The six houses behind the soap plant were actually hidden gold. They had a 2.0 percent rent-to-value factor at the close of escrow. That number would go even higher with time. In case you need a memory jogger about rent-to-value, here's what it is: The rent-to-value factor is the monthly rent divided by the total value of the house. In this particular case, the young man bought the entire property (six houses) for the total price of $135,000. That includes the lilac fragrance that permeates the air every evening when the factory fires up the soap vats during the graveyard shift.

Let's look at the dollar picture here. The six houses are earning $450 each, or $2700 per month total. Four out the six are rented to HUD tenants with guaranteed rents. The other two could easily be the same if the owner wants to. Here's another way of looking at dollar returns: Each house is earning 24 percent of its total value annually. The value or purchase price of each house is $22,500. Rent = $450 per month × 12 = $5,400 annual ($5,400/$22,500 = 0.24). Can you see that a 24 percent rent return means that each house will earn its entire cost ($22,500) back in just slightly over four years? It would take 4.16 years to be exact.

If you have a nose for making money, you should be starting to smell lilac fumes about now. Many folks get cold feet when they see the soap plant bubbling. They somehow put on their investment blinders. They never scratch the surface to find the shiny gold underneath. Anytime an asset generates enough income to completely pay itself off in just over four short years, you should be very interested in that asset. They're not all that easy to find. When you find one, don't pass by without a thorough investigation.

Profits Come from Monthly Cash Flow

When I was telling this story to an investor group, a woman asked this question, "How can I tell if it's a good deal or not? You haven't told us what the down payment was or what the monthly expenses and the mortgage payment cost." The answer is that it doesn't matter much, unless of course, something is terribly out of whack. In this particular case, I happen to know the cash down payment was $18,500 (13 percent), which means the mortgage balance was $116,500. This was an excellent deal.

Even with high-leverage deals like this, it's quite easy to structure the financing (sometimes interest only) in a way that will allow the owner to enjoy a very respectable cash flow, starting on the first day of ownership. It's also very common with these types of rental houses to earn handsome profits, even if the property doesn't appreciate one thin dime. The reason is that the property is a cash machine almost from the beginning. You've actually acquired your own private little gold mine, so to speak. Each month you can mine out fresh green cash.

Let's suppose you're able to net $500 each month from the "soap factory houses." That adds up to $6,000 the first year. Your return on cash invested is 32 percent. You have also acquired approximately $100,000 worth of depreciable property (income shelter) in addition to cash flow. Forget about the future of the houses for a moment and only consider the income stream. For the next 10 years, even with very modest cost-of-living rent increases, it's a very good bet you'll be netting $10,000 annually by the end of the term. It's not the least bit difficult to visualize this one small property generating $100,000 worth of cash and tax benefits in 10 years. Even if you sell the houses 10 years from now at the same price you paid, that's not bad. I will assure you, lots worse things can happen to investors.

An important thing to remember here is this: When you are lucky enough to locate income properties that have a rent-to-value factor of 1.5 or above, it's like the old gold miners say, "You're startin' to see some pretty good colors!" Stay with the deal and figure it out. There's an excellent chance you're standing very close to a cash flow spigot.

Houses Are the Vehicle to an End

Investing in rental houses and being a landlord are not my goals. They never have been. Owning rental houses and being a landlord are the vehicles that are taking me to my goals. To keep focused on the big picture means that I must keep the vehicle separate from the goals. Stated another way, I'm in the housing business to make money, not simply to own a bunch of properties. In fact, as much as I like owning houses, my underlying motive sounds almost selfish. They are the best vehicles I know of to take me where I wish to go. Houses are not the end for me; they are the means to an end.

Understanding this makes it much easier to make sound investment decisions, I believe. Let me explain it this way. My goals and personal dreams are probably quite similar to every other investor's out there. Without mincing any words it means making money.

When you understand that your goals are the objective and not the vehicle, it helps you zero in on an investment plan that makes the best use of your time and resources (money). For example, in my case I needed to quickly develop monthly cash flow without paying a ton of cash for my properties (which I didn't have). Only certain types of properties will provide cash flow, so that's where I directed my energies. Also, another one of my goals was to quit my regular W-2 salary job. That set up tight restrictions on my time limits because I had to have money to live on within a couple of years from the time I started buying properties.

Well-Financed Houses Are Very Low Risk

In terms of investment risk, I'm talking about the risk of losing your assets. Rental properties, like the ones I own, are about the safest kind of investment you can make. Naturally, you must avoid paying too much and taking on too much mortgage debt. Residential renters are a much easier bunch to attract than commercial tenants, plus everyone needs shelter. Houses are considered a basic necessity of life. The danger of anyone taking your investment houses with any equity is almost nil. If you buy them right and structure the financing so your tenants will pay them off, you'll be very well rewarded for all the efforts it takes.

11

The Riley Street Houses:
How to Earn $429,000 in Nine Years, Moonlighting

In this chapter you will learn about:

- Reading the classifieds to find owners who want to sell
- The advantages of seller financing
- Questions to ask in your first conversation with the seller
- Ten key ingredients that made the Riley Street houses a good deal

It was rainy, cold, and wet when I drove up. Only die-hards like me would look at ugly houses on a day like this. The classified ad sounded good. I might point out that I look through my local real estate classified ads every day that I'm home. It's just a habit, but I think every investor should do it. Over the years I've hit several home runs by reading the classifieds. Readers may recall my Haywood Houses, which are detailed in Chapter 2 of *Investing in Fixer-Uppers.* That turned out to be a barn-burner project.

The Riley Street property consisted of eight run-down houses on two adjoining lots in the older section of my town. The location was a good "Johnny lunch bucket" area. Blue-collar service workers from a nearby hospital complex lived there, as did several deadbeats who thrived on stiffing landlords. I discuss their rent-paying habits a bit later. Sellers will often forget to tell buyers about the paying habits of their cherished customers when they're trying desperately to sell the property.

It was nearly dark when I drove up, so I parked about half a block away and walked back to the property. Snooping around like a detective, I discovered that the back door of one vacant house was open. After I kicked it rather gently, it opened and I tiptoed in. It was a filthy two-bedroom, but I was pleased with the space and layout. It appeared that maintenance funds were scarce, since the toilet had overflowed several times with no apparent cleanup attempt. At any rate, I discovered six of the houses were two-bedroom units, about the same style, and the other two were smaller, one-bedroom units. No question about it. This was the kind of property I lust after and crave.

I Always Read the Classifieds

The Riley Street houses are exactly the kind of properties I'm searching for, and in this case my local newspaper was enough to get me excited. If you're an active real estate investor, you should always read the local classified ads—income property for sale. It's not too often that you'll buy the property listed in the ad; however, making contact with income property owners pays big dividends.

My local classified section will generally have several properties for sale by owners. These are situations where the property isn't listed by a licensed real estate office. I have found that many owners will attempt to sell their property themselves before listing it with an agent. Obviously, they are trying to avoid paying a commission. However, talking directly with owners offers many potential benefits to me that far exceed saving a little money on commissions.

Big Benefits of Seller Financing

Without question, the Number 1 benefit of working directly with owners is being able to find a seller who will carry back (finance) a large portion of the sale price. That's worth a great deal because it automatically brings with it additional benefits that can really sweeten a transaction. Here are a few additional benefits I look for:

1. Softer terms than those offered by institutional lenders (banks or mortgage companies)
2. Excellent opportunity to buy back the mortgage at a large discount later on
3. Less restrictive terms, like no due-on-sale clause
4. Easy-to-modify terms of mortgage in emergency situations, such as a high-vacancy period
5. A seller carryback mortgage (financing), which is highly desirable when you decide to sell the property because buyers always pay more when they can assume good financing without needing a new bank loan (mortgage)

Following is a copy of the Riley Street ad that appeared in my classifieds:

INCOME PROPERTY FOR SALE
(6) 2 Bedroom houses
(2) 1 Bedroom cabins
2 Separate city lots
Priced at $245,000. Owner will carry 2nd mortgage
with only $40,000 cash down. Property will show
positive cash flow. Principals only. Call
123-555-7890 (out-of-town telephone number)

Making a Telephone Contact

I called the owner who told me the location of the property. He also advised me to see his tenant-manager if I wanted to inspect the units inside. He gave me some general information about financing, loans, owner expenses, and so on. I've learned after many years of experience that dollar numbers given over the telephone can be much different from the same information when it is provided in written form. Also, it's quite common for many expense items to get left out of telephone conversations. Therefore, I listen, I take a few notes, and then I write to the seller asking for written answers to my questions. This is a good technique because it doesn't require the seller to think too much. I handwrite my informal letters so that all the seller has to do is fill in blanks. For example: "How much was last year's tax bill? $_____ Please provide a copy of the tax bill for my records."

My short, written questions about the property are designed to get straightforward answers. Mostly, they're about mortgage terms, taxes, expenses, rents, vacancies, who pays what utilities, and so forth. Always ask for a copy (front sheet only) of the fire insurance policy. This will show the value an insurance company places on the property. Also it's very important to always ask: Do all the units have separate meters? And who pays what utilities and how much?

I always ask for a mortgage payment stub, county tax bill receipt, and copies of owner-paid utility bills for several months (copies of canceled checks are OK). Providing this information is no big deal for legitimate sellers. Still, it is just enough commitment to keep them honest. Also, the information provides me with more details about the property during the purchase negotiation.

The Riley Street houses would be a good moneymaker in my judgment. Each unit had separate utility meters. Tenants paid all utilities. There would be approximately 75 percent private seller financing. I would need to formally assume one existing bank mortgage. I had previously determined that rents for all eight units were substantially below current market values. There were two primary reasons for this: First, the owner was renting at below-market rates because he reasoned that with low rents he wouldn't be bothered with too many repair calls. Many landlords use this strategy. I personally don't think it's a good one. Repairs should be made as needed, especially to older units; otherwise, the property runs down and no longer attracts decent renters.

The second reason is that out-of-town owners seldom know the current rent values unless they take the time to study them. Most out-of-town owners are simply not informed about local rents. As a result, most properties I purchase from out-of-town sellers are charging too little for rent. That's a big bonus in helping me achieve quick cash flow. Remember this when you are involved with nonlocal owners. It can be a real bonus.

Draw a Sketch Showing Apartments and/or Houses

You needn't be an artist to draw squares on a paper. Let each square represent a unit. Write the address of each unit in the square. Then ask the seller to write in next to each square the tenant's name, amount of deposit, amount of rent, and the rent due date.

I find this little exercise is well worth the effort. Why? Because when someone takes the time to write information down on paper, their memory suddenly becomes much more clear. The combined rents given to me over the telephone were $2,500 for all units. When I added up the squares on the sketch, they totaled only $2,350. When I questioned this discrepancy, the owner told me he thought the rents had already been increased.

The obvious lesson here is this: Talk is cheap and hard to recollect. With written documents, the words are there as a permanent record for everyone to see. My informal letter, my asking questions, and my sketch showing each unit as a square were mailed to the out-of-town seller. I informed him that as soon as he mailed the sketch back, along with the requested information, I would quickly prepare an offer and send it to him.

Structuring Your Written Offer to Purchase

I got very excited when I learned the Riley Street houses were all substantially under-rented (rents were lower than they should have been). Naturally I'm very familiar with rents in my town, and therefore I knew that two-bedroom houses should fetch $450–$475 a month, not $325–$350, as the seller was receiving. It doesn't take a rocket scientist to understand that if you can purchase property based on its gross income of $2,500—which should be $3,600, if properly maintained—you are acquiring a real financial bonus starting out.

In my letter to purchase the Riley Street houses, I wrote:

Rents = $2,350 per month or $28,200 annually, according to the written information you sent me. Thanks for correcting what you told me on the telephone ($2,500).

Re: Tax bill—you're right! Something is haywire with the amount you indicated to me on the telephone. California Proposition 13 makes taxes roughly 1% of the sale price per year. For example: on a $100,000 sale you can figure Shasta County taxes will be about $1,100 per year. Current mortgage payments are $1,005.56 and $435.89, total = $1,441.45.

I will submit the following offer:

Price: $210,000

Cash down (net to you*): $20,000

I will assume (take over): $102,800

2 exist. mortgages: $57,700

Seller will carryback a note (3rd mortgage): $29,400

10 years amortized: Payments of $390.57 per month

*Net to you means I'll pay 100% of escrow fees. Any credits I receive for my share of rents or deposits will not reduce the $20,000 down payment. The carryback mortgage will be adjusted instead. This way you get the full $20,000 you told me you needed.

Can close as fast as you wish. Also, I will provide any personal credit information you need.

My contingency is that I give final approval within 3 days after I'm allowed to see inside and walk-thru with you or your manager.

JAY   Tel. 123-4567

Finalization of the Offer

After several more telephone conversations about the property and my offer, a compromise agreement was reached with the following changes:

1. Sale price increased by $5,000 to $215,000.
2. Cash down payment increased to the sum of $25,000.
3. Seller agreed to carry back third note and deed of trust (mortgage) on property for approximately $35,000.

4. Payments $550 or more per month, 10-percent interest. (Pays off in 7 years, 9 months.)

The only added contingencies on my part were that all heating and cooling equipment had to be in good working order at the close of escrow. Also, I would verify all tenant records, basically the rents and deposits held by the seller.

The offer was also subject to my being approved to assume the existing bank mortgage, which required "formal assumption" because of the due-on-sale clause. Since my credit was excellent, I knew there would be no problem.

The only thing unusual about my offer was its net-cash-to-seller offer. That means that the seller got the full $25,000 cash down payment. No deductions were to be made for his share of closing costs. John needed $25,000 cash, and I agreed.

The seller's carryback mortgage would be adjusted (reduced) by the seller's 50-percent share of escrow expenses, title insurance, rent proratings, security deposits, and any other costs customarily paid by sellers.

Rent-to-Value Factor of the Riley Street Houses

With a total sale price of $215,000, let's review the amount of rent each unit earns in relation to its value. First, I assign a value to each unit:

Six 2-bedroom houses = value $30,000 each. Total = $180,000

Two 1-bedroom houses = value $17,500 each. Total = 35,000

Average rents for the two-bedroom houses were $340 per month. Therefore, rent-to-value = 340 ÷ $30,000 value = .0113 per month or nearly 14 percent annual rent return (.0113 × 12 months = 0.1356).

Average rents for the one-bedroom houses = $230 ÷ $17,500 value = .0131 per month or about 16 percent annual rent return (.0131 × 12 months = .1572).

Anything over a 1.0 rent-to-value ratio is very good: 1.0 percent equals a 12 percent annual rent return on the unit. For example, a $50,000 house that earns $500 per month rent is earning a 12 percent return (12 months × $500 = $6,000 ÷ $50,000 house = 12%).

Fix-Up Costs Itemized Estimate

After looking at the inside of the Riley Street houses, it was time to estimate my costs for fix-up. Once you've done this a few times, you'll become quite good at estimating these costs. Nothing teaches you better than having to pay all the bills yourself.

Table 11-1 shows my estimate of costs and repairs for the Riley Street houses:

	Each Unit	Extension
1. Exterior paint	$500 average cost	$4,000
2. Fencing repairs—rear/side		1,000
3. Remove junk autos (2)*		300
4. Chip-seal, oil, and gravel driveway*		
5. Parking areas—light grading		3,200
6. Landscaping—general		2,000
7. Interiors—painting	$400 average cost	3,200
8. Kitchen upgrading (including) A. Faucets/sinks B. Formica tops for 50% of kitchens C. Lights/electrical D. Linoleum flooring E. Electric ranges (4)	$400 average cost	3,200

Table 11-1. Estimate of costs and repairs for the Riley Street houses (continued on next page)

	Each Unit	**Extension**

9. Bathroom upgrading (including)
  A. Tub/shower converter kits
  B. Shower stalls
  C. Tub enclosure—plastic
  D. Toilets (4)
  E. Linoleum flooring
  F. Valves and stops
  G. Fans and vents
	$350 average cost	$2,800

10. Carpet replacement (includes padding)*	$500 average cost	$4,000
11. Doors and windows	$225 average cost	$1,800
12. Garage doors (4)*	$350	$1,400
13. Electric washer and dryer	$200	$1,600
14. Coolers (3)	$500	$1,500
15. Wall heating upgrade (5)	$200	$1,000
Total		**$31,000**

*Outside contractor work

Table 11-1. Estimate of costs and repairs for the Riley Street houses (continued)

My cost estimate to fix up the Riley Street houses was $31,000. The next question is obvious. Where will I find the money? Some questions are tougher than others. First, let's break down the costs. Some jobs I may do myself. Others, no way. And several items require contractor help. Here's a breakdown:

Outside help contractors	$8,900
Remainder	$22,100
Total cost of fix-up job	$31,000

The remainder is the labor and materials. On average, labor runs about 70 percent of most fix-up jobs. However, with the Riley Street property, I figured a little less because of some higher-priced materials. My estimate was 35 percent for materials.

Thus the job broke down like this:

65% labor	$14,365
35% materials	$7,735
Total	$22,100

This means that if I elect to do the labor myself, I'll save $14,365 on the job.

Always Determine How You'll Make a Profit

It's paramount to know how you'll earn a profit. The best way to do this is to write it out so you can look at the numbers yourself. I call this my cash flow chart (see Table 11-2). You will notice that I allocated the fix-up costs ($31,000) over a 17-month period. I estimated it would take me between one year and 18 months to turn the property around from its run-down, filthy condition to charming and homey.

Notice that my rent increase projections are modest (approximately 4 percent annually). This is very reasonable. It's also approximately the same amount of rent increase allowed by HUD. Remember, income projections should be believable and realistic.

You can draw a cash flow chart for any number of years you feel are necessary. In this case I felt 10 years was plenty. "But Jay, it shows only nine years," you say. That's what happens when a serious buyer shows up. The property sells and all accounting immediately stops.

You'll notice on the last line (bottom), at the end of nine years, I'll have collected $99,645 positive cash money if my projections are correct. You needn't count quarters from the laundry room here. Remember, this chart is merely a road map for direction. The main purpose is that it makes you plan and project the future. This way, you're not operating by some seat-

Plan Years	1	2	3	4	5	6	7	8	9
Unit Address									
Riley Street	5 Mos. 1991	Annual 1992	1993	1994	1995	1996	1997	1998	1999	2000
Income $	12,000	40,860	45,000	46,800	48,600	50,570	52,680	54,600	56,800	59,100
Vacancy (10%) + non-coll. losses	1,200	4,090	4,500	4,680	4,860	5,080	5,270	5,460	5,680	5,910
Operating income	10,800	36,770	40,500	42,120	43,740	45,680	47,410	49,140	51,120	53,190
Mortgage payments (3) $1,992/mo.	9,960	23,900	23,900	23,900	23,900	23,900	23,900	23,900	*17,280	17,280
Taxes/Ins.	1,500	3,600	3,800	4,000	4,200	4,400	4,400	4,600	4,600	4,600
Utilities	250	600	600	700	700	800	800	900	900	1,000
Acctg/Legal	500	600	600	700	700	800	800	900	900	1,000
Routine maint.	600	2,040	2,250	2,340	2,430	2,540	2,630	2,730	2,840	2,955
Net rents	(2,010)	6,030	9,350	10,480	11,810	13,240	14,880	16,110	24,600	26,155
Upgrade costs	10,000	21,000	—	—	—	—	—	—	—	—
Cash flow	(12,010)	(14,970)	9,350	10,480	11,810	13,240	14,880	16,110	24,600	26,155
Accum. cash flow	(26,980)	(17,630)	(7,150)	4,660	17,900	32,780	48,890	73,490	99,645	

* A third carryback noted paid off.

Table 11-2. Cash flow chart

of-the-pants strategy. You'll be very surprised how close you can come with your estimates with a little bit of practice.

Selling Out After Nine Years

Time whizzes by when you're having fun. You just get the property up and running smoothly and bang!—in comes an offer you can't refuse. That's what happened at Riley Street. The offer was for eight times the gross rental income, which was about right for the time. These houses would sell for 11 or 12 times gross rents today because the need for affordable housing is much more critical. At any rate, there's no need to nudge too close to the hog line. A good, reasonable profit should always be the goal. You may recall that the purchase price was $215,000. Let's take a peek at what nine years of ownership can do.

Sale price, $470,000

(8 x gross rents) Rents = approx. $4,925 per month = $59,100 annually

$50,000 cash down (approx. 10%)

Seller carryback note ($420,000 Wraparound note)

[All Inclusive Trust Deed (AITD)]

Underlying mortgages (2)

1st mortgage balance, approx. $72,000

2nd mortgage balance, approximately $43,000

3rd mortgage *paid off* in 7.75 years (remember)

Seller equity $305,000

I Can Offer Attractive Financing

8.0 rate, monthly payment will be $3,400 or more per month

Term, 20 years, then all remaining balance is due

With these "soft terms," buyer sees cash flow of $1,525 per month.

Buyer's monthly rents = $4,925

Buyer's mortgage payment = $3,400

Buyer's cash flow, $1,525

Here's how Jay comes out with a seller carryback mortgage:

Payment receivable from buyer, $3,400 monthly

Underlying mortgages (Jay pays)

1st mortgage = $1,005.56

2d mortgage = $435.89
                   —————————
                   $1,441.45

Net payment (Jay keeps) $1,958.55

Jay's net payment is an annual amount of $23,502. Looking back at the cash flow chart, you'll notice I didn't reach this amount of income until plan year 8. That means I unplugged toilets and collected rents the first seven years for less money. Now all I need to do for my money is run to the mailbox once every month in my pajamas and pick up my check.

Riley Houses Are Good but Not Exceptional

Riley Street was pretty much what I consider run-of-the-mill. I didn't do anything spectacular other than operate the property. Without consideration for tax-sheltering benefits, which obviously saved me big bucks, take a peek at the obvious benefits from start to finish. These are my earnings:

Cash down payment to me, $50,000

Since I paid $25,000 down, my net equals $25,000 cash.

Accumulated rents from operations, $99,645 (see cash flow chart)

Net equity seller financing carryback mortgage (wraparound), $305,000

Total value of these items at closing, $429,645

Over the next 20 years, I'll take in (receive) payments of $816,000 ($3,400 x 240 months)

My net share to keep for myself will be approximately $571,000

Both 1st and 2nd underlying mortgages will be paid off during 20-year seller financing term.

A million bucks ($1,000,645) for just one junky property!

Not bad money for eight junky houses, wouldn't you agree? How many of these properties will you need to make you financially happy? Not many.

10 Key Ingredients That Make the Riley Street Houses a Good Deal

1. Oddball leper property—eight older houses on two city lots in residential zoning. Not popular with many investors because of zoning.
2. Run-down condition, unsightly, yet no major damages.
3. Excellent location for rental units. Near schools, hospital, and shopping.
4. Long-term, EZ-pay financing (75 percent private notes).
5. Fix-up work, mostly do-it-yourself type. No major problems.
6. High-demand affordable rentals. These types of units are very scarce in my town.
7. Quick cash flow generators because of existing under-market rents.
8. Out-of-town owner was not knowledgeable about value potential or local rents.
9. HUD fix-up funds available for this property. HUD willing to pay 50 percent of fix-up costs, although I elected not to do HUD rehab with this project.
10. Property can be held long term or sold for quick profits. There are no financial restrictions.

As you search for cash flow properties, keep these 10 items in mind. They'll serve you well in finding your own Riley Street.

12

How to Negotiate with Great Results

In this chapter you will learn about:

- The importance of establishing credibility with the seller
- Skills you'll need to negotiate the deal successfully
- The three most important items you'll ever negotiate
- Verifying the facts with the income property analysis form

There are several good financial reasons to establish credibility with a seller. However, none is more important than persuading him or her to finance the sale or at least a large part of it. That's called *seller financing* or a purchase money mortgage. Seller financing is a benefit that can make real estate investors rich in a short period of time. Before we discuss some negotiating techniques to accomplish this, let me first share something Dale Carnegie said. It puts the right spin on the buyer-seller relationship: "There is only one way … to get anybody to do anything ... that is by making the other person want to do it. ... There is no other way."

The very first thing I do when I hear about a property that becomes available, assuming I'm interested, is to begin what I call detective work. Sometimes my broker, Fred, will perform this task, but it took him four years of my coaching before he became snoopy (skilled) enough to suit my taste. Brokers and sales agents typically don't do the exhaustive research or snooping around that I insist must be done.

Develop the Right Skills

The biggest difference between most agents and me is that they accept the word of sellers as being mostly true. I accept it as mostly exaggerated and often untrue. It's never considered true until it's proven to me. I'm not trying to be overly critical here, but you must never forget this important fact of investment life. Once the escrow closes and everybody gets paid, it's you, alone, by yourself, who must live with the deal you signed. If somehow you've failed to uncover the true property expenses and it turns out they're considerably higher than you were led to believe, you alone are stuck. That's the reason I learned to become a very snoopy house detective early in my investment career.

One of the best methods for negotiating is what I call the "Columbo Technique." Lieutenant Columbo is the cigar-smoking detective on TV with the wrinkled raincoat. He doesn't appear smart enough to ever solve a homicide case, yet he solves them nevertheless.

If you get an opportunity to see a rerun, watch Columbo solve a mystery. Observe how he does it. Let me offer you a little preview of what to watch for. First of all, you should observe that Columbo is never intimidating or threatening. He never appears to be competing with anyone. Yet, in his own special way, he quietly and forcefully moves directly toward his goal, which of course is solving the mystery.

Real estate investors can negotiate in a similar fashion with equally successful results. You'll notice that Columbo always has a specific reason for everything he does. His questions are always supported by clues or information he develops. His attitude is courteous and often seems apologetic when he needs to ask the tough personal questions. He always gathers his information in such a manner that he doesn't intimidate his list of possible suspects. In fact, most of them even go out of their way to cooperate with Columbo because he's courteous and seems genuinely concerned about their needs. Notice how all the villains in Columbo episodes are steadily pressured into accepting surrender without putting up much of a fight (I've never seen Columbo use a gun). The reason is that the detective develops the facts and confronts his suspect with hard, undisputable evidence that makes the conclusion obvious. He does it all without allowing his personal emotions to interfere.

Columbo's Techniques Are Very Persuasive

First, before you start arbitrarily changing or negotiating terms and/or conditions, make sure you can show the reason why. If you can't, the reason is probably not valid. Still worse, when you can't, it will severely damage your credibility.

Second, it's important to listen to the other side. You can answer yes or no if you train yourself. But listening to others will provide you a wealth of knowledge and information that will help you structure offers and counteroffers. People love to talk. If you're a good listener, you'll be very popular with most folks. Columbo is very good at this. Often suspects tell him enough to hang themselves, which makes his job much easier.

Third, never get emotional! Don't be critical, and above all, never talk down to anyone. If you humiliate, embarrass, or ridicule, you'll lose all chance of negotiating a winning deal. Even sellers who are about to lose their shirt won't do business with someone who intimidates or tries to overpower them. Courteousness and understanding are two of the most powerful tools in your negotiating kit. Use them generously; they'll pay big dividends. Once again, Columbo is a master at this.

You Must Win the People First

Consider this following exchange between a seller (owner) and a potential buyer. Both are complete strangers to each other.

"Mr. Buyer, why are you offering me 30 percent less than my asking price?"

"Well, sir, the reason is because I know that sellers always mark up their sale price because they expect the offers to be less. Obviously, you can still accept my offer because I think it's much closer to the real value of your property. Your price is way too high."

If you own a nice property (in your opinion) and you've worked your tail off to make the payments, then a buyer comes along, a total stranger to you, and tells you your property is worth 30 percent less than your asking price, what do you immediately think of the buyer as a person? Chances are, most of the answers are not printable here. People don't like to be told their property is worth less than they think. It's human nature to become upset and negative, even if it's true.

Columbo never tells his suspects anything that would upset their relationship or stop the flow of information between them. In the end, they always wind up giving him all he needs for a conviction. He wins without shouting matches, embarrassment to others, or making enemies along the way. These are excellent skills for any negotiator.

Avoid Game-Playing If You Want Real Benefits

Arbitrarily cutting the asking price is game-playing. If the price is truly too high, obviously it needs cutting. However, you should have a defensible reason to suggest the cut. If you have done your homework and can reasonably demonstrate why the purchase price should be lower, then your lower offer may be acceptable; otherwise, it's probably not.

When your offer is considerably less than the asking price and you can't explain the reason, it becomes difficult to keep negotiations productive. It's like saying to the seller, "You really don't know what your property is worth, but I do!" If you mean it that way, you'd best be prepared to show the seller exactly why.

I like to consider the terms I'm negotiating as if each one is a bullet in my negotiating gun. I have many bullets. If I shoot blindly at everything—that is, attempt to change everything in the contract to suit me, like asking for a lower selling price, smaller payments, reduced interest rate, longer length of term, less down payment cash, and perhaps even a different closing date—am I just wasting my bullets hoping to hit anything I can?

The Three Most Important Items You'll Ever Negotiate

Here's some advice you should underline! It is worth big bucks to every small-time real estate investor. In fact, if you become good at this, you can quickly move up the financial ladder from small-time investor to big-time cash flow tycoon.

The three most important items you'll ever negotiate for are the right purchase price, the right amount of debt service (monthly mortgage payment), and the length of time to pay off the debt. You can give everything else away if you need to, but you must get these three items within the acceptable range.

Negotiating Is Much Easier with Facts

My chief negotiating tool is called an "income property analysis form." What it does is enable you to develop a financial picture of the property as you fill in the blanks. It's a simple form that shows you the financial profile of the property and approximately how much it will cost you to operate the property should you become the owner. It also helps eliminate most emotional issues between the buyer and seller. With my property analysis form, both sides can work together filling in the blanks.

Sometimes a seller will argue that he or she only pays X number of dollars each month for expenses. You are certain that the numbers are short or his or her memory is fuzzy (that's a common seller affliction). When the analysis form is filled out correctly, with the assistance of the seller, it's difficult to argue facts. Generally my form has a tendency to jog the seller's memory. You'll find a copy of the form in Appendix B. Don't buy a property without using it to figure out the true operating costs first.

Always Allow the Seller to Participate

You may wish to watch a couple of Columbo reruns in order to get the hang of this. Pay particular attention to how the lieutenant uses a nonaggressive, low-key approach to uncover the facts. He's never pushy, and he never accuses anyone of not telling the truth. Above all, he works hard not to alienate his suspects. Don't misunderstand here. I'm not saying that sellers are suspect. However, just like Columbo you must verify all information. Don't forget, the truth is always verifiable. Loose words may not be.

I always ask the sellers to help me gather the information I need to fill in the blanks on my income property analysis form.

After all, sellers should know better than anyone, since they operate the property and pay the bills. My experience shows that sellers will generally provide accurate information about the gross income. But beyond that, they begin to develop forgetfulness. For example, on line 2, hardly any seller I've ever purchased property from admits to having vacancies. When they do, it's very rare, they claim. The truth is, vacancies are all too common with every landlord.

This nonsense usually ends after I ask to see their 1040 tax form (Schedule E). Hardly any property owner tells the IRS the same dollar amounts they present to me. It's quite similar to comparing the taxpayer's automobile mileage reported on his or her income tax return with the mileage given to his or her auto insurance company. Strange as it might seem, many folks drive 10,000 more miles on their tax returns. The same thing happens when negotiating income property expenses.

Verify the Actual Expenses

Most real estate agents do not understand what it actually costs to operate income properties. If you ask them for a percentage figure, most will give you a number far below what the expenses actually turn out to be. There are two basic reasons for this. First, and probably the biggest, agents have little or no experience paying the bills, so they don't really know. Obviously, they must rely on what sellers tell them. Second, if they did know the actual expenses and told their prospective clients, they might never sell another income property in their lifetime. From an agent's standpoint, knowing less serves them better. If you doubt what I'm telling you here, search through any multiple listing and try to find complete financial information.

You'll always find the income numbers complete, but expenses are another story. Most often, the agents don't fill in the blanks. They either don't know or don't want to know. Keeping the expense information hidden or vague makes the property more attractive to buyers.

I have found what works best is to have the seller provide evidence (proof) of all expenses. The checkbook register and expense journals will generally provide this information. Expenses to verify are utilities, management fees (if the property is managed by someone other than the owner), repairs, maintenance, and property insurance payments. I also want to see the county tax statements. In California, taxes are adjusted approximately 1 percent of the sale price when a property is transferred (sold).

No One Reports Too Much Income to the IRS

It's quite common for investment property sellers to be overly optimistic about their rental income numbers. For example, in my Oliver Street property, which I discuss in Appendix B, 12 × $3,115 = $37,380 annually. If the seller's 1040 tax return, Schedule E, shows rents of only $30,000 for the taxable year, my question is, what happened to the other $7,380? My guess is vacancies and credit losses (nonpaying deadbeats).

Obviously, transitioning properties might have gone through rent increases since the last tax filing, which is fairly easy to determine. The important point I'm making here is that you should never allow less than 5 percent for vacancy loss and less than 5 percent for uncollected rents and "skips." With lower-income properties, the percentages are often higher.

No One Manages and Repairs for Free

I've had property sellers tell me that there are no management fees or maintenance and repair expenses on this property—they do it all themselves. My first reaction, which I try to keep a bit low key, is to ask, "Will you continue doing it for the same price after I become the owner?" I've never had a single taker yet. Then I ask, "How much would you charge me to manage the property if I buy it from you?" No one has ever told me less than 10 percent of the total gross income per month. Most wouldn't take the job at any price. After a short discussion, they generally agree that my 5-percent management allowance on line 7 is, indeed, quite reasonable. After all, who will do it for less?

No one has ever developed a method for doing repairs and maintenance without spending money. When things break, it costs money to fix them. Painting, roof leaks, yard work, carpet cleaning, and patching walls are just a few of the maintenance and repair activities necessary to keep income properties doing what they're supposed to do—generate income.

At the very least, you'll spend 10 cents of every rent dollar collected for maintenance on older properties. Don't include capital items like new carpets, coolers and roofs. That's not maintenance. Repairs like broken doorknobs, cracked toilets, and broken windows will cost you 5 percent. Those things are repairs. Remember, these are the numbers I use on my income property analysis form. I consider these bare minimums. I rarely have any difficulty convincing sellers. Quite often their own expense records, tax returns, and 1040 Schedule Es, will show far more was spent than I've estimated.

13

Turning Motivated Sellers into Bankers

In this chapter you will learn about:

- The limitations of institutional lenders
- Why most sellers are willing to help finance the deal
- Five reasons seller financing is best
- How to reduce your mortgage payments for the first few years

Most folks who seek my advice are do-it-yourself real estaters. They acquire a house here and there and might do several deals each year. That's exactly what I do. It just so happens that I jumped on the fast track for several years, and my numbers built up rather quickly. As they say, I was on a roll. My point is that I'm still a one-house guy and a do-it-yourself investor, as opposed to Donald Trump, who, I understand, does real estate too.

Seller Financing: It's the Best Your Money Can Buy

Almost without fail, the single and most frequent question I'm asked at my seminars is "How do you finance all your properties?" My short, quick answer: "I mostly do seller financing." When I tell people that, they stare at me or they just look up at the ceiling. Somehow they don't seem satisfied with my answer. I suppose the reason is that most folks automatically think that banks are the only legitimate source for financing the purchase of real estate.

Customize to Fit the Deal

Almost every real estate book written and most of the roving gurus who teach seminars about investing expound on the benefits of fully amortized institutional financing. Certainly these can be excellent loans when they fit the deal. However, I must tell you that there is no way on earth I could have ever acquired all the rental properties I own today and developed rapid cash flow without the aid of sellers who were willing to finance their properties for me. For one thing, many of my prize properties, meaning best cash flow producers, would not have qualified for regular bank mortgages for many different reasons. Most often because of the age and condition of the property and sometimes because a foundation didn't quite measure up to current building codes. Banks don't like properties that don't look nice or smell too good. Of course, those kinds happen to be my specialty.

I think seller financing is often misunderstood because it's so simple. People tend to think that transactions are no good if they are not complicated and if they don't hurt. Just try to get a new loan today on a junky property. You'll understand exactly what I'm saying. Seller financing is structured primarily on common sense. Conversely, some of the new mortgages banks are offering these days don't make any sense whatsoever, especially when they start talking about points and a low LTV (loan-to-value).

Please keep in mind, I'm talking investments or income-producing properties, not your personal residence. The purpose of this chapter is to give you a realistic answer to the often-asked question, "Why is seller financing better for do-it-yourself fixer-upper investors?" As I explain the reasons, I think you will agree with me that owners who sell you their properties can also help you achieve your long-term goals much better and much faster than banks. I shall also attempt to clear up several myths or misunderstandings you might have about seller financing.

Will Rogers said, "The trouble with most folks is not that they know so little, but rather that they know so much that just ain't so." An important part of making big money in real estate comes from doing those things that really pay off and ignoring the hearsay stuff. Learning the difference quickly will make your bank deposit day a more pleasurable event—something you can brag about.

Five Reasons Seller Financing Is Best

Seller financing is almost always the best way to go for five basic reasons. I list them first, and then explain each:

1. It's always available.
2. It's cheaper than institutional financing.
3. It's more flexible.
4. It has better terms.
5. It's discountable.

1. Always Available

Owners who wish to sell generally want to be cashed out—that is, paid off. This most frequently happens when buyers can qualify for a new bank loan or have enough money to pay cash. Buyers are likely to consider cash-outs for premium types of properties, "red-ribbon deals," where they are highly motivated and seriously want the property. Good credit or a rich buyer is required. Generally speaking, older properties or run-down houses will not qualify for high-percentage loans. A loan-to-value (LTV) of about 60–70% is about tops. This means a buyer needs more cash for the down payment or the seller must carry back part of the financing, even if he or she doesn't want to.

Best Deals Come from Motivated Sellers

I buy properties when the sellers are motivated. Quite often, I'm the only buyer making an offer, so I have no competition. Most of the properties are run down and old, quite often both. Banks arc not interested in providing mortgages for old run-down properties. When they are, they insist on shorter-term notes, higher interest rates (worse yet, variable interest rates), points, credit checks, appraisals, and closing fees.

With seller financing I normally pay minimum down payments (10 percent) and structure terms to fit the available cash flow generated by the property. Banks couldn't care less about that. I don't pay points, appraisals, credit checks, and closing costs. I never have to wait three months for loan approvals either. Also, I don't want my payments going up just because the prime rate does. Finally, sellers can always finance the deal if they wish to sell badly enough. Their doors are always open. I recall a few years back when banks would not provide money for mortgages at any price. Because sellers financed most of my deals, I was able to keep right on buying.

2. Cheaper

Financing costs have a lot to do with real estate profits. If you've ever sold properties during a period of high interest rates, then you understand exactly what I mean. Income property is always higher risk; therefore, financing always costs more at your local bank or thrift. For real estate do-it-yourselfers like me, cheap financing is synonymous with cash flow. The reason I decided to invest in real estate to begin with was to make money for me, not the financial institutions. When you learn how to reason (negotiate) with sellers about carryback financing on the sale of their properties, you eventually become very skilled at it. It simply takes practice, but it's worth the effort.

Sellers Will Carry Long-Term Notes for Income

One big advantage for sellers is that buyers can pay a higher price for properties when the financing is less expensive. Many mom-and-pop sellers prefer bigger notes for retirement income. When we talk about discounting later on, I explain how large face-value notes with soft terms (soggy paper) can turn out to be very profitable for investors also.

The next topic to discuss with sellers concerns interest rates. Many sellers will tell you something like this: "I'm willing to carry back a note (mortgage) on my property, and I'll do it for 2 percent less than what the bank earns." Most sellers don't really mean that, and here's why: They believe that when the bank charges 7.0 percent interest on a mortgage, the payments are all theirs to keep. Obviously, that's not the case. The bank has all sorts of expenses like fancy office space, trained employees, utility bills, and so forth.

Most sellers have none of these expenses. The bank also pays its depositors 2 percent or so to get the money in the first place. If sellers truly meant they would be willing to carry financing for 2 percent less than their bank earns, I'm afraid they would be very disappointed when they see the first mortgage payment.

3. More Flexible

Seller flexibility is directly related to the motivation to sell, which is extremely important. Generally speaking, banks are not motivated, although they can be in special situations. Mostly what happens is they get all bound up by regulations and their own operating procedures. Often they cannot help themselves even when they know that being flexible would be better for them. Several times during my investing career I've hit rough sailing (financially) with my rental properties. I've been able to renegotiate cheaper monthly payments when my vacancy rates shot up over 20 percent. Several of my early seller carryback owners even extended the payoff dates on their notes for modest concessions on my part. Only 10 percent of my seller carryback notes have due-on-sale clauses, and very few have late payment charges.

Sellers Don't Want Their Property Back—Ever!

Most owners who sell to me don't want their real estate anymore. They want a steady monthly income. The point I'm making here is that they are happy to work with me because I'm honest and I treat them fairly. Banks, on the other hand, don't give any extra points or consideration for being honest and fair. Even dealing with foreclosures, most bankers have little flexibility because of bank policies and operating procedures.

With private sellers who carry back mortgages, you've got some options. Nine times out of ten, you'll find that sellers who have financed properties themselves will do almost everything within reason to avoid taking the property back. I've had several sellers completely rewrite their notes in order to help me through a tight money period. Sellers who hold notes can act very quickly because they understand their success (receiving their monthly payments) is based entirely on my success. More often than not, banks are simply not flexible enough to do what's best for themselves, let alone do what's good for you. It's important to remember that with seller financing common sense generally prevails.

4. Better Terms

Over the years, easy loan terms have been very important to my investment program. I like mortgage terms that fit the property, rather than terms that fit the lender's program. For example, when I purchase a run-down property, it's quite likely the rents will be very low. Often, after paying my normal down payment (10-percent average), financing the 90-percent balance can easily exceed my rental income unless I can negotiate special terms from the seller. Motivated sellers will do this. Banks won't.

One technique that has worked well for me is to make reduced mortgage payments during the first several years. Later on, as my rents move up, I will gradually increase the mortgage payments to make up for the earlier reduced payments. This arrangement is not the same as a normal variable-rate mortgage from the bank.

Let's say for example, I negotiate a $100,000 carryback note (mortgage) at 9.0-percent interest with payments of $800 or more per month until paid. To begin with, the interest portion of the first monthly payment is $750. The principal payment portion equals $50. Here's the typical variable-payment mortgage plan I ask for, which is normally acceptable to most sellers I deal with:

- Years 1-3   Mortgage payments $600 a month
- Years 4-6   Mortgage payments $700 a month
- Years 7-10   Mortgage payments $800 a month

| – Years 11-13 | Mortgage payments | $900 a month |
| – Years 14-16 | Mortgage payments | $1,000 a month |

After year 16, payments are reduced back to $800 per month until the mortgage is paid in full. Please note, there are no accruing interest balances added to the principal even though the payments do not cover interest during the first six years. The payments are simply "made up" for or added back on during the later years (11–16) when my rents are expected to be much higher. The seller in this example still gets his average payments of $800 per month during the life of the loan. Obviously, the buyer (that's me) gets easier payments to handle in the lower-income years.

You Can Design Your Note to Fit the Deal

In addition there are absolutely no limits to creativity with private-party notes. You can customize your notes to serve the individual needs of both you and the seller.

Advanced students sometimes ask me about imputed interest or the at-risk rules regarding private-party notes. Yes, there are some rules one must follow, but what I'm telling you here will work just fine for most new investors. When you're ready to draw up your note, it's always advisable to check out the tax consequences. Meanwhile, this chapter is about making money with seller carryback financing. If you don't make money first, you won't need to worry about tax consequences.

5. Discountable

Here's a typical scenario. I'll purchase a fixer-upper property, and the seller and I agree to a seller carryback note for $100,000. The note is designed with "soggy terms" (weak, nonrestrictive terms). Let's say we both agree to a 6.0-percent interest rate, a 20-year payback period with payments of $550 or more per month, and a balloon at the end. The note will have no prepayment penalty, no due-on-sale clause, and no late charge. This note would not be a good candidate to sell. The terms are far too weak to have much commercial appeal. This is especially true when the security happens to be older run-down houses and the down payment amount is only 10 percent to start with.

Timing Counts for Bonus Profits

Let's say five years whiz by and circumstances change. The seller passes on to his greater reward, and the note ends up in the hands of his only living heir, his young nephew. Young Tommy likes the $550 monthly income, but he also knows he must wait 15 l-o-n-g years before he can get his hands on any sizable amount of cash. Young Tommy lusts for more cash right now. The note balance is still nearly $97,000, but Tommy's been told by local mortgage brokers that his note is not very marketable—soggy terms, they say. Not only that, but when the property securing the note was sold, the down payment was only 10 percent. Note buyers would like more equity to begin with. Sounds like Tommy might be stuck with $550 monthly payments for another 15 years.

But wait! Young Tommy really needs the cash right now. His old Subaru just quit running. There it sits, dead in the driveway. Tommy loves new Firebirds. His best friend has one. It's only two years old, and it's a real beauty. By the way, it's worth big money to me to know everything I can about my note holders like Tommy (age, likes, financial situation, jobs, etc.). Buying these soggy notes back, after you originally drew them up with weak terms, can be a very lucrative business. The fact that you negotiated well with the seller and you got him or her to agree to the "soggy terms" in the first place now makes it very easy to buy your own note back at a substantial discount. Isn't this fun? You're going to fall in love with this technique when you do one.

Help Yourself Most When Helping Others

Here's what you might do to help poor Tommy. Immediately run to your nearest Firebird dealer. Test drive that new fire-engine-red beauty sitting on the showroom floor. The sticker says $40,000, but you know you can buy it for $35,000. Drive it out to Tommy's place. Park it next to his broken down Subaru, and just leave it running. You won't have to ask twice to get young Tommy to drive around the block a couple of times. When he gets back, you can start talking. Here's what you say, "Tommy, you're a smart man. How would you like to own this brand new Firebird? All paid for, plus I'll even give you a year's worth of spending money, say $10,000 cash right now, today. It's all yours if you'll just tear up your note with my $550 payments. This way, you get a car now, and you don't need to wait 15 long years for your money. Besides, you could even be dead by then. I bet 15 years from now, Firebirds will cost $100,000 or more, assuming the world don't end before then!"

Guys like young Tommy are an impatient breed. Odds are in your favor that you'll leave the Firebird and a check for $10,000 right there in young Tommy's driveway. Your total cost is $45,000. You might even finance the car through your local credit union if you need to, but look what you've done. You've just bought your own note back for less than half its face value. In terms of making money, this is not a bad day's work. Obviously, not every situation works like my storybook version; however, I'm sure you'll agree with me that if you even come close to deals like this, you're headed down the millionaire trail.

Buying Properties with Multiple Loans

I often do one-on-one counseling. People come to visit me for counseling when they need a little extra help. For example, some are interested in knowing more about how much work is required on an average fixer-upper house. We most always visit my fix-up crew in the field for a firsthand look. New investors are always surprised to learn that most of what we do is not nearly as difficult as they imagined. As is always the case, people learn a great deal from actually seeing for themselves.

One such counseling student wanted my help with financing techniques. Bob made several trips to Redding before we were finally able to make his transaction come together. When we finished, however, it was a real dandy.

Bob had already signed a purchase contract to buy an older apartment building (fixer-upper type) for the total price of $280,000. His major concern was about the four private notes secured on the property. The seller had seriously milked the building and was currently behind on several of the note payments. Bob was advised by his local banker that it's very risky business to assume or take over four private notes. She explained to Bob that banks hardly ever would allow more than two notes or mortgages to be secured on a property. A first mortgage and sometimes a second, but that's their limit. She said, "It's bad business, and it's far too risky." The banker also told Bob that any of the note holders could start foreclosure on the property because the apartments were so run down. "That's one of the major security provisions in the trust deed," she said.

Bankers Will Never Understand Entrepreneurs

Because my investor student was new at the game, the banker's advice frightened him. Bob and I determined that if the apartments were fixed up, they would easily be worth $400,000 based on the current income. Fixing them would be a breeze since Bob was a building contractor who could do almost all of the work in his spare time.

Our final offer was accepted—$20,000 cash down, and Bob would take over the four existing notes (all legally assumable) with long-term due dates and fairly low interest rates. The loan amounts were $61,000, $52,500, $40,260, and $75,400. The seller agreed to carry back a new fifth note for the balance of $30,840, all due in 10 years but with a subordination clause that allowed Bob to refinance without paying it off.

Here's what the bankers don't understand—the four private notes were all carryback financing from sales by previous owners. None of them wanted the apartments back, especially since they were progressively more run down. The current owner simply milked the rents and did no upkeep. All they wanted was their money. The banks were even more worried now because Bob had never owned apartments and therefore had no landlord experience. They can easily imagine what could happen to their notes if Bob doesn't fix the apartments or worse yet, allows the tenants to take over. They have good reason to worry.

Here's what we did shortly after closing escrow. Bob traded $38,000 worth of telephone company stock for the first mortgage note of $61,000. The trade eliminated a $575 monthly payment. The holder of the second note, $52,500, rejected our discount-for-cash offer.

The note holder for $40,260 gladly exchanged it for a small one-bedroom mountain cabin and fishing boat-trailer setup Bob and his wife owned. That trade eliminated another monthly payment of $400. Shortly after these transactions, Bob was able to secure a new loan of $100,000 for the purpose of fixing up the apartments and paying off the old fourth note of $75,400, with only $45,000 cash. That's a 40 percent discount. This payoff eliminated another $700 monthly mortgage payment.

$216,660 Equity for Bob's Effort

When the dust had all settled, Bob owned fixed-up apartments worth $400,000 with three mortgages totaling $183,340. The new financing was enough to pay for all the fix-up materials and give Bob back part of his original $20,000 down payment.

When you begin negotiating for properties that have multiple notes involved, the first thing you should do is ask for copies of all notes and trust deeds or mortgages. Deeds are public records; notes are not, so you must ask the seller. Carefully check the terms. It's good for you if they are assumable, which means they have lots of payments remaining (long term) and low interest rates. Next, try to learn all you can about the note holders (beneficiaries, they're called). Are they young, old, rich, poor? Do they have financial problems? And so on. This information is important because it determines their motivation to sell. Sometimes you can make arrangements for discounting these notes at the same time you are acquiring the property. However, I much prefer to do it later, sometime after I'm already the owner. As you can see, private notes or mortgages offer a great deal of potential for making big money. What might be risky business to bankers can be a high profit opportunity when you learn how to make these customized transactions work.

The Many Faces of Profit-Making

This stuff works extremely well. Older properties with seller carryback financing in place can be your source of some very lucrative profits. If your goal is to acquire cash flow properties, as I suggest, and you support the proposition that real estate investing is basically a long-term path to financial security, here's my recommendation to you: Look for properties where sellers will participate in the financing. I've found that my biggest profits and cash flow properties come from deals where sellers are willing to carry back a large portion of the mortgage debt with terms that work well for both of us.

PART 3

Becoming Wealthy, Staying Wealthy

14

Silent Wealth-Builders: Compounding, Leverage, and Control

In this chapter you will learn about:

- The dangers of playing the appreciation game
- The benefits of depreciation and compounding
- How to get the most bang for your buck with leveraging
- Full control means less risk and more options

There are many people who seem to think you can't make money in the real estate business without appreciation. That's absolutely false. The fact is, you can profit very handsomely without any appreciation whatsoever when you add value the way I do. I like to think of appreciation as the icing on the cake or the special bonus I get for being in this business.

Many wannabe real estate tycoons simply don't understand where the big profits come from. Flipping or selling houses in an appreciating market is often quite profitable, but it generally falls short of the big money most investors dream about.

Appreciation—It's the Icing on the Cake

Appreciation should be a wealth-builder's helper, not the whole program. If you view it as a bonus or the gravy, then you needn't worry about short-term up and down real estate cycles.

Developing properties that produce a solid monthly income will effectively remove all the pressure of having to sell. Many investors who buy, fix, and sell find themselves strapped for cash with overloaded Visa cards and a mailbox full of late payment notices. In order to save themselves from total financial meltdown, they're forced to sell out under terms far less desirable than if they had money coming in every month. With monthly income flowing in, they'd have the freedom to keep their property through up and down real estate cycles without being forced to sell at the wrong time. Selling in a low cycle can cost you $40,000 on a $100,000 investment. You don't want many sales like that.

As a rule, when real estate is hot (top of the cycle), it's not at all difficult to sell properties for 120 percent of the normal price. However, when the cycle hits bottom, 80-percent sales are quite commonplace. On a $100,000 deal, selling can be worth up to $40,000 when you're in the right cycle. Cash flow earnings of 12 percent are a reasonable expectation for investors who buy run-down properties and add value to them. By comparison, if you could deposit $1,000 a month in your savings account at 12% interest, it would take you over 20 years to become a millionaire.

Remember, selling property, especially when you're just getting started, is something like digging a hole and then filling it back in. This is because the very minute you sell a property, your investment vehicle stops earning money. Cash flow properties, on the other hand, will give you a choice of whether or not to sell. By the way, if you sell, any gains or profits you might make are immediately exposed to the tax collector. Obviously, paying taxes and building wealth don't work very well together.

Playing the Appreciation Game

The biggest problem for real estate investors who bet the ranch on appreciation is that there might not be any. Worse yet, what happens if property values drop? Real estate is a cyclical business—prices and values go up and down. Betting on short-range appreciation is like shooting craps; you can sometimes double your money overnight, but you can also lose the whole shooting match just as quickly.

Reaping the benefits of appreciation without having to be on a rigid time schedule is a much safer strategy. Real estate almost always increases in value over time. For example, a three-bedroom, single-bath house in Sacramento, California, cost about $20,000 brand spanking new in 1968. It reached a high value mark of $181,000 in 1992, and then dropped to $139,000 in 1994. The value stayed pretty much at that level for several years, and then shot up again. For short-term house flippers, most of the 1990s were down the toilet. However, over the long haul, the same house has appreciated at a rate of $5,225 every year since it was built.

If you plan your investment strategy so that you can keep properties long term, rather than selling them quickly for short-term goals, you'll end up a whole lot richer than you ever imagined. The reason for this is because you will have positioned yourself to enjoy the powerful moneymaking benefits of long-term compounding.

Tax Shelter Benefits Add to Annual Compounding

As I mention in Chapter 5, depreciation is the magic that causes your property to show a tax loss but still generate a net cash flow income. The reason for this is that Uncle Sam allows investors to deduct, as an expense item, a percentage of all things that wear out, such as buildings, coolers, refrigerators, and carpets. This expense is like a phantom expense because you don't need to write a check to pay it the way you do for the plumbing bill. The cash benefits come from two sources. First, the depreciation expense shelters the property income from taxes. For example, if a rental property generates $2,000 positive income before the $4,000 depreciation deduction is added, then for tax purposes the property will be reported as a $2,000 loser.

Second, that same $2,000 loss from operating the property can be used to offset $2,000 worth of positive income from the owner's salary or from other positive income he or she has. When you acquire investment properties that have quick-depreciating assets like coolers, stoves, carpets, drapes, and land improvements, depreciation can add up to a sizable expense item every year. Tax shelter benefits can easily be equivalent to another 12-percent interest on your investment or so, which adds to your annual compounding.

Leverage Is How the Rich Get Richer

High leverage can make you wealthy faster than any other tool in the bag. The idea is to borrow as much money as you can to put

with your own small down payment (sometimes none) to purchase income-producing properties, which you will own and
control 100 percent. For example, 90-percent leverage is where I
purchase a $100,000 building, paying only a $10,000 down payment and signing a $90,000 promissory note for the balance. If
the property earns $10,000 annual rents, then the return on my
down payment is 100 percent. Obviously, that can be good or
bad. If expenses are $4,000 and the mortgage payments are
$7,000, I will be earning 100 percent, but still losing my shirt.

Leverage is a double-edge sword. Safe leverage is the kind
you want. In this particular case, if you could increase rents to
$12,000 or negotiate a mortgage that costs only $5,000 annually,
you'll be earning $1,000 on your $10,000 investment. A cash
flow of 10 percent with 90-percent leverage is a very respectable
return.

Full Control Builds Wealth Faster

I have long held the notion that one of the most important reasons for investing and operating income properties yourself is
that you have maximum control over your investments. You
alone make all the decisions. It's you who gets to collect every
dime of income your property generates each month. You
decide who will live on your property, when to make improvements, and, of course, when to raise the rents. Naturally, it's you
who writes the checks for expenses too, but you control them.

I can't speak for others, but I like to invest my money in
things I can touch or kick. Houses and apartments fill the bill
perfectly. I also like to invest my money where I'm the boss.
With personal ownership, if something goes haywire, I have all
the controls to fix it. More importantly, I won't be a victim of
someone else's goof. If somehow you've got the wild idea I'm a
control freak, congratulate yourself. You're paying attention.

Total control particularly applies to financing when I purchase properties. Most older fixer-upper houses should not require new bank financing. As I mention in previous chapters, always try hard to get sellers to finance the sale, since owner financing is flexible and cheaper. If you buy economically priced properties (medium to medium-low range), most people should be able to afford to rent or buy from you. Conversely, if you buy high-ticket properties, you will limit the number of people who can do business with you.

If you buy right, meaning you don't overpay, and if you avoid buying properties in single-employer towns, like sawmill towns, you will always be able to maintain steady cash from rentals. Also, when you are in a position to customize terms for your resales, such as offering low down payments, options to purchase, and wraparound financing, you will always have business. Even a roller-coaster economy won't bother you too much because your moderately priced properties will service the largest percentage of the population. This way, you'll always have an income.

For example, in my hometown, I invest in moderately priced rental houses. Roughly 80 percent of the renters can pay $600 per month to rent a two-bedroom house. You don't have to be a genius to understand that if I purchase houses I can fix up, rent out, and make a profit renting for $600 a month, I'll soon collect most of the rent money in town. Steady income puts you in total control of your houses.

Although no investment is 100-percent fail-proof, I have found that houses like the ones I own are as close to fail-proof as I need them to be. Once I learned how to purchase houses so that the mortgages would be paid off by my tenants over a long period of time, the only real risk to me was right after the purchase, during the first several months or so. That's when the deadbeat tenants leave during the night with your refrigerators, and the expenses are the highest because of clean-up and fixing. After that, the risk disappears. Rents go up every year while the mortgage payments remain the same. Naturally, the cash flow locks in safety.

When you compare owning income-producing houses with the other types of investing we've all heard about, the former has much less risk and lots more control.

Danger of All-in-One-Basket Investing

One of the primary reasons I like to invest in several smaller properties rather than one huge complex (multiple unit apartments) is that I can maintain much better control. Obviously, if cash flow were not my highest priority, single-family (detached) houses would likely be my choice for maximum investor control.

It's quite simple to explain. A single tenant living in a detached rental house will rarely muster up enough steam to mount any serious tenant rebellion. Also, illegal activities are much easier to apprehend and eliminate with small rental properties.

It's not uncommon in the larger multiple apartment complexes to have tenant strikes, sticky-fingered managers, and even drug dealers conducting more nightly visits than Domino's Pizza. Worst of all, rent protests and other tenant uprisings are much more commonplace in today's society. A recent newspaper article cites a case involving 67 tenants who joined together as a group to sue their landlord in small claims court. In case you don't know, attorneys are generally not permitted in small claims court. I hope this building owner is well versed in his own rights as a landlord.

Here's the bottom line, folks: Investors need to consider a bit more than simply owning rentals today. I suggest you also think about control over your assets for the long term. It might seem more profitable to have one giant apartment building, as opposed to scattered units, but that could suddenly change for one of the reasons I've mentioned here.

With smaller rental properties, tenants generally live isolated from one another. They don't have their noses in each other's daily affairs quite so much. Also, with smaller properties you generally won't need on-site managers. You might have an unofficial overseer instead. But remember, sometimes a lousy manager is the problem.

I realize economics favor the multi-units. To begin, the unit price generally gets cheaper as the size increases. That's the good news. However, you must balance economics with being able to manage what you own. I like to think of my smaller properties as watertight compartments—like on a large ship. Each compartment can be shut off from the rest, so problems can be quickly contained with minimum damage. Using this approach, it's likely I can always save my ship from sinking when a storm blows in.

15

Oliver Street: Jay's Fast-Track Investment Model

In this chapter you will learn about:

- The top 10 benefits that determine a property's profit potential
- How being "snoopy" helped Jay find Oliver Street
- Creating cash flow by leasing with an option to purchase
- Converting your equity into cash with half sales

Making fast profits as a real estate investor doesn't happen by accident. You must plan to make it happen. Oh sure, I'm aware of a few lucky folks who happen to purchase a property at just the right time in an appreciating market and then flip it for a healthy markup. I've done that myself on several occasions, but those deals are mostly about luck, as opposed to planning and skill. What I'm about to tell you here is not about luck or speculation, and the outcome is quite predictable.

To begin with, you must look at real estate investing in terms of the benefits it will provide for you. Think of each property as a vehicle taking you to the benefits. When you focus on the benefits that earn the money, it automatically steers you to the kind of properties you should look for. Your goal should be to search for the kind of properties with many profit-making benefits, not just any property that's available for sale.

Years ago I learned that there are only two good reasons to be an income real estate investor. They are income and profits. I want nothing to do with properties that won't provide these for me. I've already owned my share of those—and they're not much fun. Benefits are what I'm looking for, and the more the better. An important thing to remember here is that investors who will learn to do things that most others won't or can't will enjoy the biggest profits in the shortest amount of time. That pretty much sums up the reason I've stuck with the house fixing business for so many years. As the infamous bank robber, Willie Sutton, used to say, "It's where the money is."

Jay's Top 10 Moneymaker Benefits

1. Buying for substantial discounts.
2. Adding value for quick income.
3. Seller carryback financing.
4. Lemonade down payments.
5. Buying back mortgage debt.
6. Leasing houses with option to purchase.
7. Increasing cash flow with half sales.
8. Cash flow from city hall.
9. Aggressive tax sheltering.
10. Selling for top price and interest income.

In my search for properties with high profit potential, I'm constantly looking for deals where I can find most of these benefits. Obviously, not all the benefits can be found at every property, and sometimes just a single benefit has enough juice to make a property a prize purchase without any others. Consider, for example, the purchase of a $200,000 property for only $100,000 (very substantial discount) or finding a seller willing to carry back a $100,000 private mortgage for just $100 per month over 20 years. Both of these exaggerated examples would obviously be too good to pass up even if the other benefits I've listed were not available. As you gain experience, you'll quickly learn how each one of these benefits can add thousands of extra dollars to your bank account. Naturally the goal is to acquire the kind of properties that can provide most of the benefits. We discuss each one in more detail as we go along.

Oliver Street—a Near Perfect Model

Oliver Street consisted of seven rental units, three single-family houses and two duplexes. Three units consisted of three bedrooms, one bath; the others were two bedrooms with one bathroom. All were situated on a large city lot, 150 feet wide by 220 feet deep. City utilities served the property.

I learned about Oliver Street from my Roto-Rooter man while he was cleaning the tree roots from my sewer lines. Oliver Street was experiencing the same problems with its sewer lines, he told me. Mr. Roto-Rooter also mumbled a few words under his breath about his problems getting paid. He said the owner told him he would like to sell the property if he could ever get it fixed up and looking halfway decent. That was my clue to visit Oliver Street.

I drove out that same evening to snoop around a bit. The layout was absolutely perfect, and my Roto-Rooter man was right. The property was a total mess. There were at least three nonrunning cars for each of the seven living units, and my guess was that not more than two would ever start. Near as I could see, Oliver Street had the potential to be a real major league moneymaker for me. Seven rental units on three-quarters of an acre with 19 cars tossed in as a bonus. It was the house-fixer's ultimate dream. Take a quick peek at the property layout sketch for Oliver Street in Appendix B. Note how the buildings are located. This is an ideal arrangement, because my customers love the privacy with trees and small yards not found in apartments. To me it means I'll never have vacancies because of the demand for these types of units.

Oliver Street Required Fast Action

It was one of those rare occasions when I felt the need to call the owner quickly rather than write, as I normally do. I found a phone number in the telephone book, but the number was TDN (temporarily disconnected) for nonpayment. See how valuable my old telephone training can be? I immediately sensed a serious problem, so I decided to drive out to make personal contact, hoping I might just catch somebody around. Luck was on my side, because the owner and his wife were both painting the inside of an empty duplex.

After introducing myself and offering a short explanation about how I came to be there (the Roto-Rooter connection), I popped the big question. The answer was a very quick yes—the property was for sale, but the price was too much. Too much for me, that is. Later the seller would come down to an acceptable price of $200,000 after we negotiated a while and got a little better acquainted with each other. The property was desperately in need of work; broken sewer lines made it stink, and the property management stunk too. The tenants were doing just about anything they pleased, and several were enjoying rent-free lodging.

The reason my negotiations were successful at Oliver Street was because the seller had almost no bargaining power. The property was an ugly, run-down pigsty, and the occupants were a perfect match. Also the income was less than I was originally told. Several tenants were doing odd jobs around the property in lieu of paying rents. The seller also 'fessed up and explained to me that he had fallen several payments behind on his first mortgage. Obviously, rents were substantially less than other units in the area because of the property's run-down condition. I didn't know it at the time, but an earlier offer on the property had fallen through because the buyer was unable to refinance the property as part of the transaction. I was told the offer was for $250,000, but to me $200,000 was still the right price. Looking back now, with special thanks to my Roto-Rooter man, I realize my visit to Oliver Street could not have been timed any better.

The property was located in an older residential part of town, but it was definitely not a slum area. I do not invest in slum areas, because it's nearly impossible to improve individual property values unless there's a major upgrade to the entire area. Also, you're not likely to find the kind of customers (tenants) you want in slum areas. Oliver Street had unusually low rents because of the property's condition. It also had lousy management. I knew that once these things were fixed, Oliver Street would command top market rents because it's a very attractive property for tenants.

Benefit 1: Buying for Substantial Discounts

"Substantial" means buying for 20–50 percent under the potential market value. Since Oliver Street was located in a decent working-class area where rents averaged $650 to $700 per month, there was great potential for increasing the property income. Substantial discounts like those I'm talking about only happen when you acquire run-down ugly properties from motivated sellers who have very little bargaining power. Quite often these sellers are milkers—owners who simply collect rents but never spend a nickel for upkeep and repairs. Finally, the property runs down to a point where only undesirable tenants are willing to live there. Obviously, you must learn a few skills in order to turn this mess around so that you don't end up in the same boat. The ultimate payback, of course, is getting rich.

Benefit 2: Adding Value for Quick Income

This benefit is very powerful indeed. Almost single-handedly you can create more income quickly. You do this by cleaning up and fixing up a pigsty property like Oliver Street, and surprisingly it doesn't take too long. The term "fixing up" actually means cleaning up, for roughly 85 percent of the job. That means that almost anyone who is willing to learn how to use a big scoop snow shovel and SOS pads can pass the house-fixer exam. Even the filthiest properties start looking good and smelling better after 10 days of paint and scrubbing. Obviously, repairs will be needed and junk cars must be towed away, but once these things are done, rents can start moving up immediately.

Most inherited tenants will not be able to afford your new rents for very long. Some will just slither away during the clean-up phase; however, a new wave of fresh customers who appreciate your efforts will begin showing up quickly. More importantly, they'll be willing to pay higher rents. How much higher, you ask? My goal for properties like Oliver Street is to increase rents 50 percent within an 18- to 24-month period. The property sketch on Oliver Street in Appendix B shows before and after fix-up rents for Oliver Street. My total rent increase is $1,540 per month or an average of $220 per house. Once you have a couple of Oliver Streets under your belt, you'll be able to start saying your good-byes down at the factory.

Benefit 3: Seller Carryback Financing

As mentioned earlier, seller financing is the great granddaddy of all benefits. In fact, four of the other benefits on my top 10 list depend on seller financing to make them work. Seller financing is a private-party mortgage between the two principals (buyer and seller) for the purchase of real estate. It's used in lieu of the traditional third-party bank mortgage to finance a property.

Properties like Oliver Street are not quite as easy to finance as your personal residence or sweet-smelling rental properties, one to four units. If the bank were to offer a new mortgage on Oliver Street, it would be a commercial loan (more than four units). The cost would be much greater, because the bank says commercial mortgages are riskier. With properties like Oliver Street, you can avoid banks and their hefty fees altogether. In many situations when mortgage money is tight, most banks will just say no to run-down properties without even blinking an eye.

Willing Sellers Are the Key

My goal is to find properties where the seller is willing to finance the sale. This becomes relatively easy to do when the bank says no and the seller wants to sell badly enough. If the seller is motivated and the buyer wants to buy the property, it's simply a matter of negotiating mortgage terms, same as the purchase price. With seller financing, unlike bank mortgages, all terms are negotiable. There are no appraisal costs, no points to pay, and no application fees. In short, seller financing can be a simple agreement between two parties about how the property will be paid for.

The matter of who has control is a big issue with me. Control has to do with terms in the mortgage contract or deed. Most bank mortgages require owners to obtain the bank's permission to sell their property or even lease it with a purchase option. Banks do this with two restrictive terms written in their mortgage agreements: One is called a *due-on-sale clause*, and the other is an *alienation clause*. With seller financing, you won't find these restrictions in my mortgages. Perhaps you're wondering how can Jay get away with that. It's easy. You must understand, my Oliver Street seller was not the least bit concerned about clauses in our mortgage agreement. His biggest concern, even fear, was that I might withdraw my offer and never come back.

Seller Financing Profits

Finally there's my millionaire-maker discounting bonus that's always possible with seller financing. In fact, it's Number 5 on my benefit list. Let me explain how sweet it is. Most sellers I purchase property from want to have all cash when I buy their properties. The obvious problem, of course, is the condition of their property. With junky-looking properties, they're fortunate to get whatever cash I give them. They simply don't have enough bargaining power to negotiate for more cash up front.

I've found that sellers who own properties like Oliver Street will always be short of cash. They don't manage properties well, and the same holds true for their money management skills. If they had more cash today, they'd still need more tomorrow. It's part of their makeup, I think. Just four months after the Oliver Street sale closed, the seller was already trying to sell the $85,900 mortgage we had just negotiated on the deal. He now needed cash instead of payments.

Because our mortgage was a third, meaning two other mortgages were recorded on the property ahead of his, many mortgage buyers were not interested in making an offer. Long-term, low-interest junior mortgages, without due-on-sale clauses or late payment fees, are typically low yield and not very attractive to most buyers. When buyers do make offers, the price they're willing to pay is often so low that the mortgage holder gets mad and just stomps out of their office. Can you guess where he stomps to? That's right—straight over to my place, where 50 cents on the dollar sounds like the best offer he's heard yet. Can you see why I call this the millionaire-maker bonus? I'm the one who negotiated the mortgage with soggy terms (weak) to begin with and now because of that, I'm the one most likely to buy it back. My Oliver Street mortgage read $85,900 on paper, but the price to purchase it back for cash was only $43,500. This stuff really gets exciting when you start slicing off your debt in big chunks like this. We discuss more debt slicing, which makes this even juicier, when we come to Benefit 5.

Benefit 4: Lemonade Down Payments

Almost everyone knows that when you mix lemons and sugar, you get lemonade. What most folks don't know is what you can get when you mix $10,000 cash and a used ski boat. The answer is a $20,000 down payment to purchase Oliver Street. You're probably wondering why on earth a seller would accept such a ridiculous offer. The answer is that he can't do any better. My offer was only the second one in two years, and the first offer fell apart.

When rental properties are allowed to run down like Oliver Street, only a few buyers will make serious offers. Competition is greatly reduced because about 95 percent of all buying decisions are based on the looks of a property. Owners of many ugly properties I've purchased over the years received no offers but mine. Lemonade offers work extremely well when sellers are highly motivated. Obviously, my seller wasn't looking for a ski boat, but accepting my offer was the only way he could get my $10,000 cash he so desperately needed. Naturally, this offer would have greater appeal during the hot summer months because we were only a short drive from the lake.

Benefit 5: Buying Back Mortgage Debt

Back to the exciting adventures of debt slicing, as we discussed earlier. Would you suppose the other mortgage holders (beneficiaries) on the Oliver Street property might have been a bit concerned about their security before I bought the property? Imagine what they must have thought if they drove by to take a look. No doubt the first mortgage holder was very upset when he didn't receive several monthly payments. You'll recall the seller reluctantly told me he was behind on his mortgage payments.

Naturally, his payments were made current when I purchased Oliver Street, but I'm certain he was still wondering how long they would stay that way. Don't forget, the property still looked like a pigsty. The only difference he could see was a new owner. As far as he knew, I could easily be another milker.

I wrote a memo to both the first and second mortgage holders asking whether they might be interested in cash rather than payments, assuming I could refinance the property. Both said they were interested but asked how much. My answer was, "As much as I can get." A week later I told them that it looked like getting a new loan was out, and I asked whether they were still interested if I could borrow from my brother-in-law. The first mortgage holder said absolutely. The second asked how much again.

You Must Always Look for Discounts

After several telephone conversations, the first mortgage holder agreed to $37,000 cash if I could pay it within 30 days. I agreed. The second mortgage holder finally called back and said she would knock off $4,000. I told her I didn't have that much. Two weeks later she called again and said that $22,000 was her final offer. She said a note broker told her he would pay that much, but she would still be out the expense of a commission. I agreed to find the money.

The bottom line for me was a $35,100 reduction for roughly two months' worth of negotiations, mostly by telephone. That's more than I made for showing up all year at my old telephone job. As I told you earlier, this stuff can be loads of fun when you look for benefits first and the property second. I'm always on the lookout for Oliver Street properties with just as many private mortgages as I can find. These discounts are real, and they add up to serious money.

I remember years ago when I first started looking for properties like Oliver Street. My real estate agent advised me to consolidate these existing private mortgages with a brand new mortgage with only a single payment to make each month. He said I could likely get a brand new mortgage and perhaps a few extra dollars to pay for my fix-up work. He also told me it would be much simpler for bookkeeping to have just one tidy mortgage payment every month. What he didn't tell me was that a tidy payment would cost me $35,100 on a property like Oliver Street. By the way, when you can eliminate $94,100 worth of debt for just $59,000, I'll bet you can find a brother-in-law somewhere if you look around.

Benefit 6: Leasing Houses with Option to Purchase

One of my good solid profit-making techniques is the lease with an option to purchase. I use lease options with my larger single-family houses to goose up the cash flow. Larger, more expensive houses don't earn nearly as much rental income as my smaller houses, based on their value. I'm not too fond of rents that drop below 1 percent per month of a property's value. For example, 1 percent per month of a $100,000 house is $1,000. That's 12 percent annually.

There are all kinds of decent renters out there who are suffering from past financial transgressions and are burdened with bad credit histories. Some even have lingering bankruptcies as they struggle along trying to mend their ways. Assuming they are truly demonstrating financial repentance and have adequate income to buy a home, these folks make ideal candidates for my customized lease-option plan.

My lease with a purchase option addresses their two biggest obstacles: a credit history that's still in shambles and not enough savings for a normal down payment. There's no way these folks can qualify for a bank mortgage, and, even if they could, they don't have any savings for a down payment. My lease-option plan can help them skip around these roadblocks. Here's how it works.

First, I allow them to lease my house for a three-year period. During this time they will be able to accumulate adequate rent credits to pay the full down payment I'm requesting. Second, I will serve as the bank when they exercise their option to purchase. Jay's bank will provide a long-term mortgage or seller financing, as we call it. I have now eliminated the two major roadblocks that would keep these folks renting apartments forever.

Switch Your Dial to Station WIFM

WIFM stands for "what's in it for me?" Every real estate investor is tuned to this station. Still, benefits must flow both ways if you wish to stay in business. We'll start with my price. Let's assume my house would be appraised for $100,000. I always ask my seminar students if they can drive down a residential street and tell me whether the houses are worth $100,000 or $110,000. Since they cannot, my base selling price will be $110,000. I'll explain base selling price as we go along.

In my town $100,000 houses will fetch $750 rents. That's not enough for me. With my lease-option plan, I can rent for 30 percent more ($225). That means my monthly income will jump to $975, which is good for me. However, on the customer side, I will give my lessee a $300 rent credit every month for 36 months. This will accumulate for most of the down payment I'm asking (36 × $300 per month = $10,800). The $10,800 plus $1,200 up front deposit equals $12,000, which becomes a full down payment credit after 36 months of leasing.

Three years is a long time to tie up a house at a fixed price—especially in a location experiencing decent appreciation. I explain this to my customers, and they mostly agree. Here's the deal, I tell them: "No other investors I know of will give you a lease, then a purchase option for three long years, and finance the deal to boot. I'm perfectly willing to do this for you, if you will help me with my greatest fear. Three years is a long time for me to agree on a fixed sale price. Since no one can predict how high real estate prices might go in the next three years, I'd be willing to split the appreciation (50/50) with you at the end of our 36-month lease. That way I feel somewhat protected if prices take a big jump. For example, if my $110,000 house goes up in value to $150,000, you will pay me $20,000 or 50 percent of the appreciation at the time you exercise your option to buy the house. Naturally, we can choose an appraiser we both agree on. The only problem I can see is that you'll need to come up with $20,000 cash to complete the sale." Most tenants will balk at the uncertainty of this provision, so I'm ready with my alternate plan.

"Pay as You Go" Makes the Plan Attractive

Most tenants realize that they won't have $20,000 in three years, so it makes them a bit hesitant. They're ready to listen to my alternate plan. Here's how it works: At the end of each 12-month period, I adjust the base selling price ($110,000) by 4 percent or about the same percentage HUD allows landlords for annual rent increases. Most folks agree that HUD doesn't gouge renters. This means that at the end of the first year (12 months), the $110,000 base selling price will be adjusted to $114,400. Two more 4 percent increases will occur, after 24 months and 36 months, respectively. With this alternate plan, there will be no appraisals and no cash shortages at the end of the leasing period. Every lease-option customer will pick this alternative plan because I've eliminated all the uncertainties. It's strictly a pay-as-you-go plan, and there's nothing that can block the customer's path to ownership.

At the end of 36 months, my house will have a base selling price of $123,735, but the down payment credits will reduce it to $111,735. This is the amount I will finance for my customer. I always offer two financing options. But suppose I offer a 20-year amortized mortgage at 7.5 percent interest with payments of $900.22 per month. That's a $75 monthly payment reduction for my tenant, who has now become an owner. As for me, I've enjoyed 30-percent higher cash flow for three years. I've sold my house for top-dollar value without having to pay any commissions, and I'm all set up to earn $105,000 in interest income. Everyone's a winner.

Benefit 7: Increasing the Cash Flow with Half Sales

Although I stumbled onto Oliver Street rather easily, it generally doesn't happen that way. My toughest job is always finding the kind of properties with all the benefits we're talking about. When I buy them, they become like family to me, and I don't like selling them. My desire to keep most properties and my serious need for additional cash caused me to consider a compromise. Instead of selling the goose that lays golden eggs and lose all my eggs, I decided that giving up some eggs was better. Hence, my *half sale plan* was born.

The major benefit of half sales is being able to convert part of your equity into cash flow without giving up the property. Oliver Street made an excellent candidate for a half sale because I had nearly doubled the property value in just two years, plus I had 100-percent control of the financing (no bank mortgages with restrictive clauses).

My rents were increased from $3,115 to $4,655 per month ($1,540), and the new property value was estimated at 7 × gross rents = $55,860 ($391,000). (See the gross rent multiplier chart in Appendix B.) After buying back the mortgages at various discounts, my equity was approximately $290,000. With half sales you are selling 50 percent of what you own. In this case, half of $290,000 = $145,000 worth of equity. Obviously, when you sell half your ownership, the buyer takes over 50 percent of the debt and receives 50 percent of the income, which was $4,655 per month at Oliver Street.

Search for Well-Heeled, Passive Investors

I always look for investors who have adequate income to handle negative cash flow: doctors, lawyers, and major league sports players who are paying the IRS big bucks on their quarterly tax returns. I offer an attractive no-money-down, long-term buy-in with management-free ownership and a promise of future profits. People whose taxes are high and who can benefit from real estate write-offs already understand that Uncle Sam will be subsidizing part of their purchase with reduced taxes. High-roller types of investors are always game for no-down-payment tax shelters without management responsibilities and potential for long-term growth. Naturally, that's my profile for a half sale candidate.

How much can I make on these kinds of deals? When my half sale closes and the dust clears, I'll have given up half my $1,400 monthly income, leaving me only $700 in rents. For the $145,000 equity (50 percent) I'm selling, my buyer will pay me $1,471.69 per month, including 9-percent interest, amortized over 15 years. With that payment, my monthly income shoots back up to $2,172 ($700 rent + $1,471.69 = $2,179.69). But hold on a minute. We're not done yet. When you own 100 percent of any property, you can't pay yourself for the services you perform. Once you sell half the property, you can bill someone else for your services.

Management fees, maintenance, and repairs will cost the new half owner approximately $575 per month. When you manage his half and do all repairs and maintenance yourself, that money comes to you. Naturally, you must continue to service your half for free. Remember, you're still the manager and the boss. You still operate the property. All you've actually done is bring in a silent partner to beef up your monthly cash flow. You'll recall I had $1,400 in rental income before this sale. Now I have a $2,747 monthly income, and I own only half the property. Is this magic or what?

Benefit 8: Cash Flow from City Hall

Owners like me who operate affordable, moderately priced

rental houses are missing the boat if they don't explore what the local HUD office has to offer. In my town, city housing has provided me with thousands of dollars to fix up my older rental units. Obviously, HUD does not build swimming pools, but it will certainly do something with cesspools—most likely it'll hook you up to the municipal sewer system.

Oliver Street was an excellent candidate for a local HUD rehabilitation grant. When I discussed the program with my local housing representatives, the popular 50-percent give-away grant was available, but since I had excellent cash flow at Oliver Street, I elected not to participate. With 50-percent grants, HUD will give you 50 percent of the total cost of rehabilitation. It decides what work needs to be done, it totals up all the costs, it selects a contractor by means of competitive bidding, and the contractor completes the job. My share for Oliver Street would have been 50 percent of all the rehab expenses.

HUD rental subsidies are available to many low-income families in all parts of the country. Oliver Street had three HUD tenants when I bought it. I've participated with local housing subsidy programs for at least 30 years, and I'm certainly aware of the horror stories. Like any story, much of what you hear is the exception, not the rule. I've had good HUD tenants who stay with me for many years and pay their share of rents just like non-HUD renters. Obviously, there are bad HUD tenants who give the others a bad name, but you should understand that it's the owners who select the tenants, not HUD. HUD's role is to supply the money. My vacancies have always been low, because I accept HUD renters. Low vacancies make for rich landlords. That's my favorite kind.

Benefit 9: Aggressive Tax Sheltering

Understanding taxes and making this understanding part of

your wealth-building strategy is worth big bucks to real estate folks like me. Many new investors pay little attention to taxes because they're not exciting like negotiating, writing killer contracts, and meeting the gang at Starbucks for millionaire trash talk. Tax dollars saved are green dollars just the same as green rent dollars. In fact, it's easier to get a $100 raise from taxes than from raising rents $100 because with tax savings you can do everything yourself. A rent increase requires your tenants to participate. The bottom line is, you should get both. Then you'll have twice as much money.

Tax laws for real estate are always changing, but, once you understand a few basic principles, keeping up with the changes is not too difficult. Most do-it-yourself investors can learn basic tax laws in about the same amount of time it takes for a wannabe plumber to hook up double-drain pipes under the kitchen sink. Income property owners with a little experience under their belt will generally agree—it's always more efficient and a whole lot more profitable when they can manage their own properties. The same holds true for owners who understand tax benefits, but the profits are bigger.

Depreciation Expenses Worth Big Bucks

I purposely look for properties where I can maximize my tax write-offs. For example, I look for personal property that is depreciating quickly and lots of land improvements because they depreciate quicker, creating bigger expenses that shelter my income. Since my basic wealth plan is adding value to properties, it only follows that I'll be replacing some of the building components in the first year or two. For example, Oliver Street needed two new roofs shortly after I acquired the property. By setting up my cost basis (books) so that the roofs were separately accounted for, I could completely write off the remaining life of the old roofs when I replaced them with new ones, using a componentizing method of depreciation. Without setting up the books correctly to start with, this $15,000 deduction would have been lost in the wind.

Take a quick peek at my Oliver Street sketch in Appendix B. You'll notice my drawing shows a 6-foot-high cedar fence around the entire property. It measures 590 feet in length and is valued at $10 a foot on my books as a land improvement ($5,900). Land improvements can be depreciated much faster than houses can be, thus creating much bigger tax deductions. Drain pipes, bridges, planters, and asphalt driveways are all land improvements. When you acquire properties that have these items, you can double and triple your normal tax deductions. Remember, tax deductions are an expense just like fixing the toilet, but you don't spend a dime to get them. On my sketch you'll notice Oliver Street was filthy rich with these kinds of deductions. Next time you visit Starbucks, take your tax code book along! You'll really impress your investor friends.

Benefit 10: Selling for Top Price and Interest Income

After 10 years of ownership, I could have sold Oliver Street for exactly the same price I had paid and still made a handsome profit. Now grab your felt pen and cross out the two words "could have," because that's not what I did. After 10 years of ownership, Oliver Street was worth about half a million dollars and had tons of income. There was no good reason to sell out unless, of course, my plan was to retire and ride off into the sunset.

My point about selling 10 years later for the same price is meant to help you understand that you don't need appreciation in this business to make a lot of money. It's the benefits that make you profits. You'll recall I earned nearly $75,000 in debt reduction before I even had Oliver Street up and running well. That's like buying a $200,000 property for $125,000 indirectly. Since I hung onto Oliver Street, I can't give you actual sales numbers, but I can show you a close estimate of how the sale would look. First, allow me to give you some personal views about financing your sales.

Earn Big Dollars with Carryback Financing

There are many investors who think that if you don't sell properties for cash, you don't have a legitimate sale. Since I've enjoyed a very comfortable lifestyle living on interest income, I must respectfully disagree. Yes, I understand the time value of money and the present value of future dollars. I can also appreciate the bird-in-the-hand concept. But I must tell you that, after years of doing this stuff, nothing is more satisfying than having your mailbox full of property payment checks every month. This can be accomplished quite easily by selling properties like Oliver Street and providing seller financing.

I like to sell properties the same way I buy them, by giving the best terms I can. Naturally, I sell for top price because my properties are in top condition. Here's how the numbers might look:

$500,000	Sale price
50,000	Down payment
51,600	Balance of existing mortgage debt
$450,000	Owner carryback (wraparound) mortgage, including $51,600 of existing mortgage debt at time of sale, payable at 7.5% interest, 30-year amortized payment schedule. Payments of $3,146.50 per month.

My $450,000 carryback mortgage would be a wraparound mortgage, meaning I would remain liable and continue paying the existing mortgage debt, approximately $740 per month.

After all is said and done, my net mortgage income would be $2,406 per month until the underlying debt is paid off in about 7 years. After that, my income jumps to $3,146.50. Today, my biggest challenge is to stay physically fit, so I continue to jog 150 yards down to my mailbox, in my pajamas, to pick up my mortgage checks.

16

When You Need a Helping Hand

In this chapter you will learn about:

- How to find and keep an excellent handyman
- The difference between an independent contractor and an employee
- How to avoid tax audits with good bookkeeping and contracts
- Common legal factors that will determine who pays taxes

At my seminars, a frequent question is, "Can I purchase run-down properties, add value, and still make a profit without doing the work myself?" The answer is absolutely yes, you can. You make the choice. You can do all the work yourself, part of it, or nothing at all. You decide your own limits, but don't forget what I say in other chapters—85 percent of fix-up work is really nonskilled work, stuff that anyone can do with the proper elbow grease. Often, the amount of money you have will dictate how much work you can hire out. In my own case, the answer was not very much.

Different Strokes for Different Folks

One of my star students living in California's high-priced Bay area made a ton of money doing this stuff, and she never picked up a hammer. What Beth did learn, however, was how the various jobs should be done, how much time they should take, and how much the cost of her materials would be. She also learned very quickly that all hired help isn't exactly the same. The labor pool can be full of sharks, so if you plan on swimming there, you'll need to know a few basics, such as who does what, where to look for the right helpers, and how to protect yourself from a shark attack.

Whether you start out with helpers or add them as you go along, you must have some working knowledge about hiring help. Also, what type of help? Should they be employees or contractors? It's not my intent to offer you legal advice, but I can tell you how to go about rounding up helpers.

If you're like me, you purchase run-down properties and do most of the fix-up work yourself. If you're successful, the day will soon come when you'll need outside help. You'll discover, just as I did, that there aren't enough hours in a day or a month to do all the things that must be done. When you find yourself working 80 hours a week, it's time to begin looking for some outside help.

Handyman—Jack- or Jill-of-All-Trades

As we all know, a handyman can be male or female. Since there's no gender-neutral term to replace "handyman," please keep an open mind as I relate my stories! In fact, one of my best all-around handyman helpers was a gal named Kathy. She worked with me for almost 15 years. Kathy did almost everything except fix toilets. She worked at my rental office; she interviewed tenants, cleaned apartments, painted houses, and did my annual HUD inspections. Although Kathy eventually became a full-time W-2 employee, she began working as a part-timer for several hours each week.

In the business of fixing houses and managing tenants, I use two different types of workers. I use workers who report to work each day on a regularly scheduled basis. They are my W-2 employees. I also use handymen who don't work every day. They work by the job. They are independent contract workers (ICs).

The purpose of this chapter is to help you understand the difference between regular employees and independent contractors. This information will help you to decide which type of worker is best for you when you can no longer do all the work by yourself.

Finding Good Help

Good handymen are an important part of real estate wealth-building. When I first began fixing up houses, handling the labor was easy. The workers and the boss thought alike, worked alike, and planned alike. And there were no labor disputes back then. I was the boss *and* all the handymen. My first four run-down houses on Pine Street were totally fixed up by me. Back then, all the help I could afford was me. Several years later "me" was no longer enough. I needed outside help to assist me.

Before I elaborate on the important differences between an employee and an independent contractor, allow me tell you how and where you might find your help. Following is an advertisement I've placed in local newspapers with fairly reasonable results.

When You Need a Helping Hand

<u>HELP WANTED:</u>
Need hard worker who wants extra monthly income,
RENTAL HOUSE REPAIRS. Approximately 20
hours per week. Will pay by the job. Must have tools,
truck & a city license. Call 123-4567 after 5 P.M.
Ask for Jay.

Perhaps you may be wondering why I was asking for help from someone who already has a job. It's for the same reason your boss assigns the biggest, most important jobs to his employee who already has the biggest workload. Busy employees are busy because they are capable of getting a lot done. People who aren't very busy probably can't be all that productive. This is a page out of Human Nature 101 called People Business.

Another good source is retired military folks. They like to work a few hours each week to supplement their retirement check. They generally ask to be paid in cash when their job is done. I will tell you now, don't make cash payments to anyone. Always write a check. I'll explain why as we go along. One big advantage of hiring ex-military is that generally these people are a bit older and have better basic skills for repairs and maintenance work. I've found that most 20-year-old kids today can't fix anything except junk cars and video games.

Another excellent way to find a handyman quickly if newspaper ads are not working is to pay a visit to a local real estate office. Ask an agent who manages property to tell you who the firm hires to make repairs on the houses it manages for clients. Generally most real estate offices will have a list of handymen they can call. I've found some very good workers this way. One important advantage to using this method is that normally the workers have already been screened. Only the good ones are kept on the list. The know-nothings and deadbeats have already been eliminated. I've found that most workers who do call-out repairs for real estate companies are always searching for more work. If you can offer them more work or more hours, they may work for you instead.

Keeping Good Help Once You've Found It

Regardless of the method you use to find a good handyman, the important thing is to find and keep him or her. You'll need to try several workers before you find the right one. But once you do, I suggest you increase these workers' pay. Not too much, mind you, but just a little more than they're getting from their other job. If you do this quickly, you'll shock them into working for you. Now they're yours for life or at least until someone else does the same thing to you. Finally, if you ever find a worker who does everything exactly the way you want it done, a worker who never complains and who works hard, works fast, and does it for reasonable pay, you need to treat him or her very well. These are the kind of workers who can help turn poor struggling landlords into rich real estate tycoons.

Paydays and Record Keeping—a Simple Task

Most handymen will ask to be paid at some hourly rate. They also want their money when the work is done. Most want cash payments, and almost all want their total gross earnings. They don't want payroll deductions for taxes and social security (FICA). They consider themselves contract workers, and most see no need to have any money withheld from their earnings. In fact, one of the biggest advantages they feel is getting paid every day, hopefully in cash. As I told you earlier, don't pay cash to anyone. Instead, write a check so you'll always have a record of the payment.

This arrangement is quite simple for the handyman, and it's also simple for the person who pays the worker because bookkeeping and accounting are minimal. Using this payment method, the payer (that's you) will need to prepare a 1099 form at the end of each year showing how much you paid your worker. Simply add up the checks, fill out the form, and send it to your worker. Send a copy to the taxing agency. Nothing could be simpler.

Hiring Is Easy—the Rules Are Complicated

Hiring a handyman to help you with your fix-up job sounds innocent and straightforward; however, there are some serious pitfalls for the novice investor, including most property owners and landlords who are just starting out in this business.

To begin with, let me start by saying that the government would like every worker to be an employee. Naturally, the government wants you to be the employer. When I say "the government," I mean both state and federal taxing authorities. The reason they like this employer-employee relationship is that they have considerable control over employers, which makes it easier for them to get their taxes. Employers are required to have special ID numbers for payroll reporting. The government says employee income taxes are the responsibility of the employer.

The employer is charged with the responsibility of collecting them and getting the tax money to the government. With employers in charge, the government gets all the workers' tax money collected up front. It never has to chase the money or listen to heartbreaker excuses about why it's not paid. Employers are required to deposit payroll taxes in the bank. Like most landlords, the government clearly understands the wise old saying about "a bird in the hand."

Many workers, especially itinerant and part-time handymen, would rather not pay taxes up front. Many don't make a great deal of money to start with and simply don't want to pay payroll taxes and wait for refunds at the end of the year. Others claim they're working for themselves and that they should be the ones responsible to the government for taxes. Many handymen simply won't work unless you agree to pay them gross earnings. These workers claim they are independent contractors working only for themselves.

Independent Contractors: Who Is and Who Isn't

Basically, an independent contractor is a person who is in business for himself or herself. That's exactly what most handymen will tell you they're doing. But all handymen are not independent contractors just because they say they are. True independent contractors have some clear and distinct differences from those who are not.

As I said earlier, most handymen want to be paid soon after they finish their job, which sounds like every contractor to me. Contractors normally want their money when the work is done. Handymen will usually ask to be paid at some mutually agreed hourly rate. For example, in my town if a handyman has any skills at all, he'll generally ask for $10 to $20 per hour. Some want more.

Receiving pay by the hour is not the normal way most contractors are paid. Employees get paid by the hour. Contractors, on the other hand, will generally bid a certain amount to do a job. After they finish, they expect to be paid in full. It's also the custom for contractors to present a billing statement that shows the services rendered, as well as the total amount due.

Employees don't do that. Employees punch the clock and expect their hourly rate regardless of the results.

Learning to Tell Ducks from Swans

As you can see from the payment methods, it's not always clear what kind of a worker you might have. Yet knowing exactly what kind of worker you have is very important. We talk about the common legal factors used by taxing agencies to distinguish employees from independent contractors in just a bit. First, I want you to be aware that most people you interview for a job will tell you they're an independent contractor and work strictly for themselves. What you must do is determine if they are a duck or a swan. Some may act like a swan, even look like a swan, but if you hear just one little quack you best beware.

What they really are will determine whether or not you must withhold taxes and social security from their paychecks. It also determines when you must purchase worker's compensation insurance. The law says that all employees must be covered by their employer's worker's compensation policy. It might seem like a good strategy to carry worker's compensation for contractors; however, it does look a bit weird because true independent contractors are supposed to have their own insurance coverage.

Knowing the Difference Can Save Your Bacon

Some say ignorance is bliss, but with handymen it can be quite expensive. If you hire a handyman worker and treat him like an independent contractor, that is, you don't withhold payroll taxes and FICA (social security) from his paychecks, chances are everything will be just fine unless something goes haywire. What generally goes haywire is you suddenly fire him or, worse yet, he falls off your roof. He could head straight to the nearest state employment office and file for unemployment pay or disability benefits. He could forget to tell the state office that you and he had mutually agreed to no payroll deductions or tax withholding. He might even forget to mention that the independent contractor idea was his to begin with. He can claim that he was, indeed, your most loyal and trusted employee. The clerk at the desk will eventually ask for your version. Think back. Do you remember what I told you earlier? In most experience, government folks want all owners to be employers and the workers to be employees. They have very little compassion for people who aren't one or the other.

As I promised, we discuss the common legal factors used to determine this relationship between you and your worker in just a moment, but first, I want you to fully understand that the deck is already stacked against you if your worker files a report.

Let's pretend that your independent contractor is judged to have been an employee when he fell off your roof. We'll also say that you were so sure about his independent contractor status that you didn't purchase worker's compensation insurance. You're in very deep trouble. Many employers cover their independent contractors with worker's compensation insurance for just this reason. In my judgment, that tends to look like you secretly harbor some thoughts that your handyman is really a big white duck rather than a beautiful swan.

Who Needs a License Anyway?

Many people wonder about this. Does an independent contractor need to have a license to be an independent contractor? The answer is "not necessarily," unless he performs a service or trade that requires him to hold a state contractor's license. For example, in California, plumbers are in a specialized trade, as are construction framers, electricians, and roofers. People working in these trades are required to have a license to do work for the general public. Most states allow a small dollar limit for work done by unlicensed persons who do minor work. In California you can perform around $600 worth of specialized work before you need a license. Obviously, owners doing their own work are not covered by this rule in most cases.

The Separate Entity Test

Handymen do not need a contractor's license to do routine repairs and maintenance work in my state. They may be required to have a city business license or permit, however. Handymen who are true independent contractors are in business for themselves. They work for themselves. They find their own jobs, they present cost estimates for their work, and, when the job is done, they hand you the bill.

Quite often you see their advertisements for work in newspapers or the Yellow Pages. They have signs on their pickup trucks, such as Sam's Do-It-All Service. Many work out of their homes or rent small office spaces. Clearly they look and act independent. If your worker just happens to be doing business as a one-person corporation, that's great. Corporations are a legal entity, so they automatically pass the separate entity test. That's exactly what a corporation is in the eyes of the law. Corporations even have their own special employer ID numbers.

In my experience, the real problem is, that most handymen don't know the legal definitions or requirements for incorporation. The best you can hope for is that your handyman has filed his DBA (Doing Business As): doing business under a trade name. That's easy enough to do at the county clerk's office. For example, Joe Smith, doing business as "The Toilet Surgeon."

Trade names clearly, more or less, indicate a separate business of some kind. All Joe's paperwork, including business cards, cost estimating sheets, and billing invoices should have "The Toilet Surgeon" printed on them as well as his city permit number, if applicable. A trade name by itself does not constitute a separate entity. You must check further to determine Joe's true worker status.

The Common Legal Factors

Try to picture a perfectly balanced set of scales with equal weights on both sides. On one side is the independent contractor. The other side is for employees. Each weight on the scale represents a common legal factor used by taxing agencies to determine whether your handyman is really a true independent contractor or an employee in disguise. This is the test the tax people will use if you happen to be unlucky enough to have a payroll tax audit.

Most audits happen when a worker files an unemployment claim or files for disability benefits and the state agency has no record of the employer. It also happens sometimes if your worker fails to pay income taxes or social security on his earnings. Most handymen will agree to pay their own taxes when you hire them. Some will even sign a contract promising to pay them.

This withholding tax problem generally shows up about three years after your handyman started working for you. The taxing agency has been receiving your 1099s each year but no matching payments from your worker. Guess who might be required to pay his unpaid taxes and social security withholdings, if the agency thinks you're really an employer? It's sickening when you guess the right answer, so let's move on and talk about the common legal factors instead.

Remember our scale with the weights on both sides. Each common legal factor represents a weight on the scale. Some are heavier than others. I'll point out the heaviest weights as we discuss each of them. Your challenge here is a simple one. Whenever you hire a handyman and treat him as an independent contractor, you must make sure you have the most weight on the contractor side of the scale.

Tools and Equipment

Independent contractors generally should have all their own tools and transportation. If you do furnish any special tools or equipment, rent them in your worker's name. You need a written agreement to do this. However, it's always better when the handyman supplies everything. He looks more like a true independent contractor. Most employees expect you to furnish everything. Try to avoid furnishing any tools.

Control

You may set completion dates, provide plans for the finished job, even stop or suspend an independent contractor who is not following the signed agreement. You cannot tell him when to report to work in the morning, when to break for lunch, or how many nails to use. If you hire an independent contractor, you are his client. The key here is this: The client may control the ends but not the means. Too much control for you makes your worker look exactly like an employee. Control is an extra-heavy weight.

Method of Payment

Don't pay independent contractors by the hour. They should be paid by the job. Let's say your handyman wants $10 per hour for building a new fence. He figures it will take 20 hours of work. Boards, posts, and other materials cost $300. This work item can be written up on a contractor agreement form like this: "Install

100 lineal feet of cedar fence, 60 inches high. Fence to begin at the northwest corner, then south to existing fence. Total price $500." Notice how I convert the hourly rate and material costs to a lump sum. When the fence is completed, the handyman can submit his bill for payment: Total due $500. I said it before, but I'll say it again—don't ever pay cash to any worker. Always pay by check. It's the only way you can get a tax deduction. Also, it's the only way to keep good records. Without proper records, you will lose any audit decision simply on the formalities.

Termination

Employees can be fired at the employer's will. Generally the written contractor agreement should provide a termination clause. I would recommend not less than 10 days' notice. Remember, the termination clause in your contract does not mean you need to wait 10 days to stop a job for safety violations or if the job is not being done according to your instructions. Let's say, in the case of fence building, your contractor is installing 50-inch boards instead of 60-inch boards as the contract agreement calls for. You may stop the job immediately for contract violation, but the termination must be done according to your contract. Always use a written contractor agreement for maximum safety. Any termination notice should always be in writing.

Service to the Public

If your independent contractor works for several businesses just like yours, he looks like a separate business entity. If he works only for you and all his earnings come from the checks you write him, he starts looking like your employee. My suggestion is to hire a handyman who has several different sources of income. In other words, he performs similar services for other employers like you. Hiring a handyman who does a variety of different jobs for real estate agents is an example of this. The more sources of income your handyman has, the more it looks legitimate for you. Don't most independent businesses you know of have lots of different clients and many sources of income? This item is a heavy weight in the factor test.

Advertising

Employees don't advertise their services. Most independent contractors do. For example, "Sam's Puppy Poop Yard Service" or "Betty's Window Cleaning Service." Read the service directory in your local newspaper's work wanted columns. In addition, many independent contractors advertise in the Yellow Pages. Employees don't usually advertise; they read the help wanted ads. They're looking to land interviews with potential employers. I think you can see the differences here; so can the taxing agencies. My suggestion is to have your handyman advertise in the free shoppers. It's cheap, and who knows, he might even find another part-time job, which will add more weight to the IC side of your scale.

Length of Service

Handyman Pete has worked at fixing up your rental houses for the past five years and has rarely worked at any other job. This relationship seems way too permanent. Unless you have adopted him, he's probably a true employee. Independent contractors usually do jobs of much shorter duration. Your contractor agreement should specify job start dates and work completion dates. The idea here is that you shouldn't have workers hired as independent contractors without specific time limits for performing the work. People who work for long periods on your property present the appearance of an employee-employer relationship. This adds weight to the wrong side of the scale if you wish to call your worker an independent contractor.

Skills or Distinct Occupation

Special skills requiring lots of training will tend to indicate independent contractor status. Examples are engineers, doctors, plasterers. People with these special skills almost always need a license to perform their work. Most folks would agree that handymen don't seem like they're highly skilled in a particular trade. This is not a deal-killer weight factor; however, if you lose some weight here, you'll need to make up the loss with some other factor.

Pay Bonuses and Insurance

Independent contractors don't get bonuses at Christmas time. Many employees do. Don't give your workers extra compensation for doing nothing. If you feel like giving, do it by adding more money to their contracts (written agreements). Regarding liability and health insurance, true independent contractors should carry their own. Who provides yours? If you are an employee, perhaps your boss does. However, if you're like me, in business for yourself, you shouldn't have any doubts about who pays for your insurance.

Store Front or Office

Employees normally report to work at your office or wherever you ask them to be. Most independent contractors I know either have a rented space or work out of their homes. As with many of these common legal factors, this single factor by itself is not heavy enough to sink your boat. If you have an audit, however, you're in a much stronger position if your worker has his own place of business. Even his house is much better than your place.

Belief of the Parties

This is a super-heavy weight. Obviously, there is no better evidence about what the parties believe their relationship is than a well-written contract between the client (that's you) and the independent contractor (that's your handyman). Not having a written contract doesn't mean you're dead if you have an audit, just as a good contract doesn't mean you'll pass either. Remember, a contract is a formality. Doing business the right way is called substance. Substance always overrides a formality. Still, just in case the weights are balanced about even, a well-written contract could easily tip the scale in your favor.

A well-written contract, like the one in Appendix A, certainly would not indicate that I have control over my worker. It clearly spells out the terms of work to be performed. Remember what I said earlier. If your handyman talks about hourly compensation, you must change his thinking to cost per job instead. The written contract should also specify who furnishes tools and your right to inspect or stop the job. It should clearly state who pays federal taxes, FICA, and state income taxes and how to settle disputes. Your independent contractor's place of business or home address should also be shown. My contractor form was approved by my attorney, but you should always have your own contract checked out by an attorney in your area, even if you use a copy of mine.

As an extra protection for myself, I've developed a special rubber stamp that I use on all independent contractor paychecks. The legal jargon says, "The person accepting my checks agrees to pay all applicable payroll taxes, including state, federal, and FICA." Again, it's not a guarantee in an audit, but it certainly gives added weight to independent contractor status. A well-written contract and clearly marked paychecks will go a long way in determining what you and your handyman are up to in case someone wants to know.

17

Managing Your Property and Your Tenants

In this chapter you will learn about:

- Why landlording skills outrank negotiating skills
- How to avoid the rent-collection, "the check is in the mail" game
- The truth about tenants and how to outsmart the deadbeats
- Why you need to prequalify your tenants before showing them around

During a recent radio talk show interview, I was asked, "What particular technique or special skill has made you the most money during your long and obviously successful real estate investing career?" That question is very easy for me to answer. I don't even have to think about it. However, my simple single-word answer always seems to surprise people.

Understandably, "landlording" doesn't conjure up an exciting image for most listeners. Still, that's my answer, and I'll stick with it.

Years ago I learned that investing alone is not enough. I had to become a skilled businessperson too. Many investors I've known over the years are rich one year and broke the next. Their lives are like a yo-yo, constant turmoil. In contrast, I've had good deals and bad deals, but my trend has always been upward.

Obviously, I know many different ways and techniques to make money with my real estate. Over 45 years or so, I've done just about everything with houses and apartments, even building from scratch. But, I must tell you right here and now, some of my most rewarding (that means profitable) deals have come my way because I know how to be a good landlord. I can handle tenants, and I know how to arrange my business affairs to protect myself and stay away from problems. I've never gone broke doing what I do. I owe that, my friends, to my business skills. My business, of course, is managing the people who live on my property.

In his bestseller, *Rich Dad's Guide to Investing*, author Robert T. Kiyosaki uses a phrase "buy, hold, and pray" describing what some investors do. He says: "Most people are not investors. Most people are speculators or gamblers. Most people have the buy, hold, and pray the price goes up mentality. ... A true investor makes money regardless of the market going up or crashing down." I agree 100 percent with Mr. Kiyosaki. That's exactly what I do.

Educate Yourself Before Jumping In

Many small-time mom-and-pop investors give up the opportunity to make a ton of money and have a wonderful, financially independent lifestyle because they never see the importance of learning landlording skills. You don't become a skilled landlord when you acquire houses. You simply become the owner. *Skilled* landlording requires some extra training.

Basically there are only two ways to learn landlording. You can learn from me or several other good teachers I can recommend, or you can learn from the tenants. I promise you right now, if you pay me 10 times more than I charge to teach you, it will still be cheaper than learning this job from your tenants.

No one is born with all the skills necessary to be a good landlord. Sometimes at my seminars, I'll ask the group if anyone would consent to having a kidney transplant performed by a wannabe physician who had only read a book or two about the operation. I'm sure you know the answer. Yet, almost the same thing happens to tenants all the time. Investors acquire properties, and suddenly they're in charge of the people who live there. They have no formal training whatsoever, and in many cases they've yet to read their first book on the subject. Many new investors start right out having tenant problems and they often get worse until something serious happens. It's no wonder we hear so many horror stories floating around.

I just love swapping landlord stories. They often reach their most gruesome detail at local cocktail parties. Everyone's got a landlord horror story, it seems, whether they own real estate or not. If you happen to be a brand new investor, you should enjoy the humor the way I do, but always consider the source. Don't let doom-and-gloom landlording tales keep you from investing or discourage you from pursuing your financial dreams.

Remember, buying ugly houses for 50 cents on the dollar takes skill. So do lease options, buying paper, adding value (fix-up), bank repossessions, partnerships, and selling for top dollar. Each are specialties and require education, and each of these specialties can earn you decent profits by itself. But none of these things will provide you with long-term wealth (the kind you hope to have) if you don't have a proper foundation to build on. When your business is houses and apartments, you need people skills and a business plan to support your real estate activity.

It's the Tenants Who Make You Rich

Let's talk about money strategies and investing your hard-earned dollars in long-term keeper properties. To begin with, it's your tenants who will make you rich. Fixing and selling properties will merely put some temporary spending money in your pocket. You needn't take my word for this; just check around. Almost everyone I talk to about this subject winds up telling me something like, "Jay, I should've never sold," or "I only wish I knew back then what I know today!" Some folks even fib a little, saying: "If I hadn't needed the cash so bad, I would have never sold my houses." For some strange reason, the same folks who tell me they agree with my long-term investing are the quickest to sell when they smell a fast buck.

Buying and selling properties reminds me a lot of my old basic training days in the army. When I was drafted, I was immediately sent to Fort Ord near Monterey, California. There was one particular training exercise I'll never forget: digging foxholes in the sand at Monterey Beach. All week long my training outfit ran double-time from our barracks down to the beach to dig foxholes in the sand. Then on Sunday, we ran down to the beach and filled all the holes back in. As an investor, you get about the same results when you buy a good property and then sell it. After everything's said and done, there's nothing left to show for all your effort.

Investing for financial independence and long-term security should be about capturing all the benefits from your investment. Selling a property provides only a single benefit, a fully taxable sales profit, and that's it. After the sale, the benefits are gone. I often hear the so-called real estate gurus recommending this buy-sell strategy. They rave about clean profits without tenant hassles. It's clear to me they're not really up to speed on how wealth is accumulated.

Acquiring the Deeds and Keeping the Benefits

On Sunday, October 7, 2001, my good friend, real estate investor-teacher Pete Fortunato, addressed 735 attendees at the Las Vegas *Millionaire-Makers Seminar*. His subject was selling properties. It didn't take Pete more than a couple of minutes to deliver his crystal-clear views about selling. In part he said, "Looking back over a span of 35 years investing, every serious mistake I've made has involved giving up my title to the real estate." That's powerful testimony coming from a highly skilled practitioner like Pete. About all I would care to add is amen!

Over the years quite a number of investment schemes have been designed for the sole purpose of avoiding tenants. Their popularity centered on easy money, no hassles, and no toilets to plunge. Stay away from landlording, the gurus will tell you. Just get the money and leave the work for someone else. Many of these so-called no-hassle strategies involve options, sandwich leasing (leasing property from an owner with an option to purchase), and selling contracts. They also mean you'll never own any real estate or acquire any deeds. The problem with these slick-sounding techniques is not so much a question of whether they work or not. The question is, where are all the benefits? Easy money and avoiding tenants are not what makes real estate investors wealthy. The benefits needed for building wealth are equity build-up, appreciation, and tax-sheltered income. These benefits are generally missing from most of the easy-money, fast-buck schemes I hear about.

You Have to Break Some Eggs to Make Some Real Mayonnaise

I'll be the first to admit that lots of strange things can happen to landlords who manage people living in their properties. If you want to achieve your long-term financial goals, there's almost no way to avoid being a landlord. It's almost impossible to hang onto wealth over any length of time if you don't own the properties that earn the money. Simply stated, when you sell a property, you also sell the benefits. You must never forget—it's the be,nefits that have everything to do with building your wealth in the first place.

In case you don't quite understand what I mean about making mayonnaise, it means there's no substitute for the real thing. Successful real estate investors don't pussyfoot around picking and choosing what they like or don't like about investing. To earn the big bucks, you must take full advantage of all the benefits real estate ownership can provide. To do this, you must own the assets and manage them wisely.

In his timeless classic, *The Richest Man in Babylon*, author George S. Clason explains the five laws of gold. "Wealth that comes quickly goeth the same way. Wealth that stayeth to give enjoyment and satisfaction to its owner comes gradually, because it is a child born of knowledge and persistent purpose. To earn wealth is but a slight burden upon the thoughtful man. Bearing the burden consistently from year to year accomplishes the final purpose." Excellent advice for today, written nearly 80 years ago.

My Top Wealth-Building Skill: Landlording

Landlording skills are a very necessary and important part of my long-term wealth-building strategy. In fact, I consider my landlording talents more important than my negotiating skills or the techniques I use to acquire properties in the first place. Let me explain why. For starters, my tenants pay all my bills and support my independent lifestyle. I also expect them to pay the mortgages on all my rental properties and pay for all the maintenance and repairs to keep the properties in good condition. In addition, they pay for my personal residence (much fancier than theirs) and of course my car, which I use to keep an eye on them to make sure they abide by my leasing rules. Finally, after everything's said and done, I own the deeds and they have only the memories and rent receipts. In all fairness, I must confess, learning to be a good landlord has been a very small price to pay for all the benefits I've received.

Time and time again, my landlording skills have enabled me to acquire cash flow properties that nearly all of my competition backed away from—great properties with temporary people problems. Many would-be buyers are scared to death when they discover tenant problems. Disruptive tenants frighten them away. Not so with me. Just knock 30 percent off of the selling price, and I'll wrestle with your tenants in a flash. Tenants don't intimidate me because they're simply no match for my landlording skills. To me they're merely temporary, short-term problems.

Remember what I said earlier about benefits: Benefits are what investing is about. Benefits will take us to the money. With unruly tenants, my landlording skills allow me to take over the seller's short-term tenant problems in exchange for long-term real estate benefits. They're likely to include seller financing, low interest payments, and a long-term, easy-pay contract without restrictive clauses to burden the deal. That's a wealth-builder trade-off I'm happy to make.

A Good Plan Prevents Vacancies and Avoids Risk

Building long-term wealth for yourself and your family should be as risk-free as you can possibly make it. The Number 1 risk for any business is not having enough money coming in on a regular monthly basis to pay the bills. If you expect to reach the investor's promised land, you must have income you can count on rather than sporadic wads of cash every now and again. I pay my bills monthly, so that's when I need the income. When you have customers (tenants) paying you their monthly rents, you're pretty much guaranteed to have the money when you need it. Cash flow removes a great deal of risk and uncertainty from any investment plan.

In order to increase my odds for success, I decided that my rental houses (my product) should be priced so that the largest number of available customers (renters) in my town could rent them. Stated another way, I wanted my houses to be within the price range of the majority of renters in my town. To do this, I would need to own houses that I could profitably rent at between $400 and $550 per month, after I did the fix-up.

I think you can see the safety part of my strategy. By targeting approximately 75 percent of all the renters in my town where affordable rental houses were already scarce, I felt quite confident that vacancies would never be a serious problem for me. Vacant houses with monthly mortgage payments to pay could have easily crippled my early investment plans because I had very little extra cash in the bank for a rainy day. The least amount of risk was very important to me.

In my town I discovered there are two major groups of people who rent houses. The first are young folks 20–35 years old. The second group is seniors ranging from 60 to 80 years of age. My town provides the younger group with mostly service types of jobs: restaurants, retail stores, and gas stations. Most seniors are living on social security checks, and about half of them receive additional income from private pensions. Approximately 75 percent of both groups can afford to pay between $400 and $550 rent per month.

Once you develop these statistics for your buying area, your investment strategy will begin to take a definite direction. Stated another way, if my purpose is to rent my houses to the largest group of potential customers (75 percent), I must develop a buying strategy that allows me to purchase, fix up, and rent my houses for somewhere between $400 and $550 per month. Obviously, if you plan to buy, fix, and sell, you must think the same way. Simply substitute the selling price for monthly rent. Once you have developed your marketing plan, you're now set to bring on the customers.

Common Pitfalls of Management

Landlords often find themselves in serious hot water with tenants because they try to inject too much logic and common sense into tenant management. Logic and common sense have their place, but they seldom count for much where legal issues are concerned. For example, it is nearly impossible to effectively force your personal living standards and ideals on your tenants—a very common mistake many new landlords make. I would advise every rental property owner to seriously think about what I'm telling you here, because it has a lot to do with keeping your sanity. What earthly good would it do you to make a million dollars from your rental properties if your tenants drive you to the nut house?

Landlording is not fun, so don't consider it a hobby. You must prepare yourself mentally to deal with your customers (tenants). You must avoid personal conflicts over matters such as lifestyles, housekeeping (inside), and moral issues. As a landlord-business person, these issues are not your business. All matters relating to their tenancy should be kept strictly on a business level.

By the way, landlords who learn to act before small problems become big ones will control most tenants. This strategy works very well for collecting rents and also for enforcing your tenant rules. Speaking of rules, many landlords have far too many rules. It's best to keep your list of rules short and enforceable, rather than long and toothless.

Rent Collection Should Never Be a Game

Contrary to the horror stories we've all heard about, most tenants who agree to rent your property will pay their rent, if you treat them fairly. In fact, approximately 96 percent of all renters, rich or poor, pay their rents even when they receive government assistance, such as AFDC or school grants. Trust me on this, I have enough tenants to prove it. The serious problems are caused by the 4 percent who don't pay, and they can literally destroy your life. It's like the old saying about one rotten apple in the barrel, and unfortunately, "destroy your life" is not overly strong language for what can happen when totally innocent but dumb landlords are matched with unscrupulous deadbeats.

Without knowing it, many property owners and fee managers allow themselves to be sucked into a silly little rent-collection ritual each month. The game begins when the tenant tells the landlord that the check's in the mail. Then the landlord starts calling every day, or worse yet, driving out to the property to inform the tenant that he hasn't received the check yet. Sometimes this game goes on for weeks, even months.

"Where's the rent?" is the dumbest landlord question in the book. It's dumb because both parties know the answer. The landlord understands full well that he or she doesn't have the rent because it hasn't been mailed yet. Obviously, the tenant knows the answer full well because he's the one who hasn't mailed it. A question never needs asking when all parties involved know the answer. It's really a form of harassment and does no good for either side. It almost automatically makes a liar out of your tenant, and there's no sound business reason to do that.

This brings us to the first rule of rent collection: Never chase the money. If you're having trouble collecting rent, I'll show you how to save your nerves and your sanity as well by using my memo system, which I detail later in this chapter. It's the slickest management tool you'll ever lay your eyes on. You'll love the way it works. I could have never managed nearly 300 tenants at the same time and lived this long without some help. Written memos are my help. They saved my bacon, believe me!

Would you rather be popular or profitable? You don't have to be a greedy person or steal candy from babies to become a wealthy landlord. What you must be is a fair-minded businessperson. "Fair-minded business" means that accounts receivables (rents) are collected in a timely manner and that your business assets (houses) are maintained properly by the tenants who lease them. See how simple this stuff is?

Landlords will not be disliked or hated any more than the supermarket cashiers or bank tellers when they demand timely rents. Everyone knows that cashiers will not allow groceries to leave the store until they collect the money. Customers expect that, and they don't hate cashiers for following the rules. Landlords who insist on timely rent payments are not any different from cashiers in the supermarket.

Rent collection is a landlord's most serious business. Quick enforcement of the rules when needed is the best method I know of to keep your tenants paying as they promised. If you have the proper paperwork (like my memos) and a good tenant file, like I suggest, you'll find it's much easier to correct a mistake (erase bad tenants) when the need arises.

Outsmart Deadbeats

In the event that you do find yourself with a deadbeat, you should know that the playing field is not exactly level. Deadbeat tenants are entitled to many freebie services, starting with legal assistance. Usually a local legal aid society or the civil liberties union is available for the asking. Also, the court system is different for deadbeat renters. For one thing, most don't pay standard fees to answer complaints the way ordinary citizens do. They are granted a fee waiver simply by filling out a pauper's form or declaration stating that they have no money to pay. The best defense against deadbeat renters is to simply outsmart them. Believe it or not, it's easy to do. Educate yourself and simply use the rules already on the books. I'm referring to your state's landlord-tenant civil laws, and of course, your own rental agreement terms, agreed to by you and your tenants when you rent them the house.

Know the Law

Civil laws will vary somewhat from state to state; however, I've found that most states are a lot more alike than they are different. Once you have developed a good understanding of the intent of the law, you'll find the laws to be almost the same everywhere. Always remember that laws are about fairness, equity, and compromise. They're not about beating the poop out of your tenant just because you own the house. Nor do they favor tenants. Laws are mostly about equity. Remember, there are unscrupulous landlords just as there are naughty tenants. It's my belief that landlords should correct their tenant selection mistakes by doing their own evictions, at least in the beginning. This will give them valuable knowledge about how the system works. You need to learn the mechanics, what forms to use, and a little bit about civil procedure.

The Application Form: What to Ask

One of the biggest problems new landlords encounter, especially part-timers, is preparing themselves mentally for the task. Just because you own rental properties, you're not automatically a qualified landlord. In fact, many property owners find out the hard way that there's lots more to landlording than first meets the eye. To begin with, although it sounds simple, you must learn how to qualify the people who will rent your property.

Landlording is a serious business when you own and operate income-producing properties. I don't mean serious in the sense that you need to worry or constantly be uptight. What I mean is that landlording is necessary for the production of income—your income.

It's very important that you learn, on paper, everything you can about a tenant applicant before you hand over the keys. This information should be required whether you rent $300-a-month apartments or a suite on top of Trump Towers. The first thing you must determine is whether the tenant can afford to pay the rent you're asking and, second, what you can do to collect the rent if your tenant fails to pay.

Let me interrupt myself here to point out that my entire

approach to landlording is to minimize personal contact between my tenants and me. My emphasis is on providing nice, clean properties and giving top-rate service for a fair price. In return, I expect my tenants to pay me the rent and to abide by the 13 covenants in my rental agreement. (See Appendix A for a copy of this rental agreement.)

There's absolutely nothing in my rental agreement that should make it necessary for much further discussion after the agreement is signed. Obviously, when a tenant rents my house, he or she has already inspected it and decided it's the place he or she wishes to live. Quite frankly, it's not even necessary for landlords to like their tenants. A landlord's obligation is to provide the best possible housing for the rent he or she receives. Liking tenants or social involvement is not part of the agreement.

Qualify Your Tenants Before Showing Them Your Property

The key is to qualify your tenants based on what they can afford, not what they tell you they can afford. As a general rule, most tenants can afford to pay about 35 percent of their take-home pay for rent. That means after taxes or payroll deductions, if they work. Older tenants and seniors can often pay up to 50 percent of their income and have no problems. The reason for this is because they have learned to budget their resources from years of experience and because they're wiser. There may be exceptions, of course. As a rule of thumb, the rent-to-income ratio must be lower for tenants with young children, automobiles, and pets. These things cost extra money. However, it's best to use the same income-to-rent ratio for everyone you rent to and not discriminate. Don't rent to applicants who do not have adequate income to pay the rent you charge (based on whatever rent-to-income ratio you use).

Have you ever made the rounds to view the model homes when developers present their annual home tours? The houses are all decked out with expensive furnishings, and the yards are landscaped immaculately. If you're like me, you begin the tour looking at houses selling for $75,000 and end up viewing those costing $350,000; it warps your value system. Your desire to own suddenly jumps light years ahead of your financial capacity. Most folks who do these tours like me are rational people. Their minds can adjust to their pocketbook without too much difficulty. But consider what might happen without this adjustment. The results would be similar to a child at the dinner table with eyes bigger than his or her stomach. Without some kind of adjustment or restriction, the child always takes more food than can possibly be eaten.

Landlords need to use this same logic when they rent their properties. Never show $1,000 houses to renters who are not qualified to pay a nickel more than $600. Naturally, they'll want the house they can't afford. Before you show a house, you must first qualify the tenant's ability to pay rent. That will dictate the property you can show them. It's just like the model houses. If you show $1,000 units to $600 tenants, I'll guarantee either you'll lose them as a customer or they'll attempt to stretch beyond their financial capacity by agreeing to rent your $1,000 house. If they succeed, as often they do, you'll be the one who has a problem. You'll end up chasing rents and listening to tear-jerker stories every month about why the rents are late or how the mailman lost the check. Unfortunately, you're also the one who's mostly to blame!

Use Memos to Enforce Rules

Over many years, I've discovered the key to easy people management (easier than most methods) is to keep emotions out of the daily management process. You'll find it's almost impossible when you visit or call your tenants every time something becomes an issue, such as collecting rents or enforcing of your rules. Lots of time will be wasted listening to excuses. Writing the tenants a memo is far easier and much less emotional than visiting tenants or talking on the telephone. With writing, you have time to think, so you don't spout off, saying things you'll be sorry about later on. With writing, you can simply state the facts, stick to business, and keep emotions out of your communication.

My memos have allowed me to oversee hundreds of tenants in a businesslike manner. Figure 17-1 is a sample of my memo asking my tenant "Carol" not to park a friend's boat on my property. When you write memos, you establish a permanent

| ONE STOP HOME RENTAL
Division of JMK Traders
PO Box 493039
Redding, CA 96049-3039 | Date _Anytime_
Subject _Commercial Use_
_85679_ |

TO: "Yard Sale" Carol
4800 Shasta Dam Blvd.
Shasta Lake, CA 96019

"Insurance Violation—Rental Property"

MEMO
LETTER

Hi Carol: Need your help!

Whoever has boat for sale on property (near your house) will need to remove it. Our commercial insurance company will have a fit if someone from there sees it (it's our landlord insurance). We are not allowed to conduct selling around rental properties—yard sales, car sales, furniture sales, etc. The reason they tell us: it brings strangers onto the property where we have private residential rentals. Liability of our tenants is involved, they tell us. At any rate, please ask owner to remove it. Obviously, we must keep our insurance to operate. Sorry for the inconvenience.

Thank you.   Bob, Mgr. for Owners

Figure 17-1. Sample memo

record. You can follow up to see that the problem has been taken care of or mail it again, marked "2nd notice." These memos will help you drink less and sleep better once you get the hang of using them. Tenants are not overly fond of them, and maybe that's why they work so well.

The memo is meant to discourage yard sales on rental properties. When the general public is allowed to visit, drive on, and browse around rental houses (multiple units), it sets the stage for problems. Yard sale browsers park on lawns, don't watch out for small children playing, and often leave junk behind (soft drink cups and sandwich wrappings). Sometimes after many garage sale shoppers visit a rental property, the tenants (other than the seller) report things missing. Generally speaking, lots of people showing up in vehicles to a multiple rental property increases the owner's liability. Therefore, we say the insurance company will not allow this activity. It works very well.

Repairs and Service

Set up your landlording business just as quickly as you can to handle service and repair calls. Establish a routine. Pattern yourself after Sears and the telephone company. They have excellent repair service operations, and both companies have lasted over 100 years. When you collect people's money for your product—your rental houses—you must be ready, willing, and able to service your customers and fix things when they go haywire. Don't use some sorry excuse like, "My husband works hard all week long, so he'll be over Saturday morning to fix your running toilet. Just jiggle the handle until he gets there and have the kids go out back." That would not be acceptable to you, and it won't be acceptable to your customers either.

Comply with Habitability Laws

Never rent your property until it's completely ready for occupancy. Sounds simple, huh? I still see investors allowing tenants to live on their rental properties before things are up to snuff. If a smart tenant moves in and things don't work right, the tenant has you hands down if he or she decides to make an issue of it. Each state has habitability rules. Know what they are, so you don't get trapped. For example, if a cooler or stove doesn't work and I decide to charge less rent so I can avoid fixing it, that's a no-no. If my tenant squawks about a nonworking appliance, the housing authority will make me fix it immediately. If it's in the building, it must work. If you don't wish to provide cool air, remove the cooler before renting the place. All systems associated with the house must work if they are present when the property is rented.

Develop Good Paperwork

Always use a rental application and, of course, the rental agreement, if you approve the application. Use applications, agreements, and co-signer agreements that are designed to provide you with information you need to know about your customers. For example, all my tenant forms are designed to help me know everything about my tenants. Generic forms are often much too general with their questions. I have excellent forms (five for every tenant who rents from me).

Split Payments for Struggling Tenants

Rents are the wheels of your investment wagon. Get your rents any way you can or you'll be left sitting on your axle. Folks always ask me whether I'd accept split rent payments from tenants. The answer is yes, if I have a decent tenant who is struggling. Usually I take partial payments that match their paydays. Split payment arrangements are verbal only; I never change my monthly rental contracts. Let me also add, I collect fairly decent-sized deposits. It's better than collecting first and last month's rent in most cases.

Interim Tenants Maintain Cash Flow

This applies to house fixer-uppers like me. Quite often when I'm fixing up several houses or a small apartment complex, the job might take me from 12 to 24 months, start to finish. If I purchase filthy, run-down units renting for only $350 because they're so trashy, my goal (after fix-up) would be to rent them for $500 per month rents.

I use interim tenants to maintain my cash flow. Gypsies are tenants who will live in my apartments while work on the property is going on. I'll give them a good deal, say rents of $400–$450 for the initial fix-up apartments. Undermarket rents, yes, but they will have to put up with my workers around them and noisy power saws. It's a good exchange as far as I'm concerned.

Treat Tenants Fairly

Wild Bill "Tycoon" Green, a seminar leader some years ago, wrote in his book, *Two Years To Financial Freedom*, "never smoke dope or sleep with your tenants." That's excellent advice, I believe, and I'll add my 2 cents' worth here. Stay away from your tenants most of the time; at least stay out of sight.

Since we're on the subject of business, any experienced businessperson will tell you that customers seldom become very close friends. Quite often favoritism creeps in if you allow customers to become good friends. What you owe customers is total fairness, not friendship. Some folks may argue with this, but when they reach 200-plus tenants like me, I'm certain the picture will become a lot clearer. I try to apply my 60/40 rule with all my customers. I'm willing to give 60 percent, if they'll give me 40 percent in return. That's enough to make me a very wealthy landlord.

Landlording Is a Business

Managing your property and tenants is a business. Treat it that way from the very beginning, and you'll be ahead of the game. Many new investors have a problem in this area when they begin buying properties. It does no good to negotiate a killer purchase price, which most investors consider fun, and then give all the money back to your tenant who sues you over a habitability matter that you weren't overly concerned about. This can easily apply to many other landlording obligations when you decide to leave operating decisions to someone else because they're not nearly as exciting as making offers at Starbucks.

When I told the radio host "landlording," I meant it with a capital L. He chuckled for a second, and then saw that I wasn't joking. As most of you know, I love good jokes, but this isn't one. When you make landlording serious business in your daily affairs, your investment life will become manageable. There's no way I could have ever acquired 200 houses without my landlording skills.

18

Selling Your Property:

Your "Pajama Money" Retirement Plan

> **In this chapter you will learn about:**
>
> - Selling for top price and interest income
> - The tax benefits of installment selling
> - The major advantages of wraparound financing
> - The additional security needed for low-down-payment sales

One of the most rewarding parts of investing in income-producing real estate comes when you eventually sell the property and finance the sale yourself. I've mentioned this before—it's called *seller financing* or *taking back a mortgage*—and it's what almost every get-rich real estate book suggests you try hard to find when you're the buyer (find a seller who will carry the financing). There are many benefits to both sides when sellers are willing to offer and provide the financing.

There are also several heavy-duty booby traps lying in wait for the unsuspecting or uneducated.

When I write about this subject, I usually refer to trust deeds, promissory notes, and beneficiaries because I live in California. However, mortgages work exactly the same way in nontrust deed states. The beneficiary is the person who gets the payments, meaning he or she benefits, and it's those payments coming to me every single month from the sale of my property that I refer to as "pajama money." The reason I call my promissory note payments "pajama money" is that I can jog down to my mailbox once a month in my pajamas to fetch my check. Nothing could be easier, and nothing in the real estate business is nearly as much fun.

Cash Sales Don't Bring Highest Profits

If you happen to be a new investor or you're just starting out, you've probably never thought a great deal about playing the role of banker when you sell your properties. Pay close attention here because I'm about to show you how to make some serious profits you might not have ever considered before. Every do-it-yourself investor should take full advantage of this lucrative opportunity, in my opinion. It's one of my favorite strategies, and, by the time you finish reading about it, it should become one of yours.

There are many who say you don't have a fully legitimate sale of your property unless you receive all cash from the sale. Obviously, everyone's entitled to an opinion, but selling for all cash may not come anywhere near the financial reward of substituting yourself for the banker and financing the deal for your buyer. Folks who support all-cash sales are always quick to point out the time value of money versus waiting to get paid. They also blab a little about the missed opportunity for those dollars that you don't have in your hand to immediately spend when the deal closes. To be fair, there's a bit of truth to both arguments. But, as is often the case, truth and profits don't always line up on the same side in the real world.

Seller Financing Seldom Involves an Appraiser

Selling your income properties with owner financing and good terms will open the door for many high-profit opportunities that would not otherwise be available with an all-cash sale or even when institutional lenders are involved. One of the most obvious benefits is the fact that you can sell for top dollar (the highest price). This happens for the same reason that almost anything will sell for more money when a buyer is allowed to pay the price over time (making payments).

A second major reason is that seller financing seldom involves an appraiser, which would not be the case with a regular bank mortgage. Even though income properties are generally appraised using the income stream method of value, hired bank appraisers can be quite conservative, especially with older properties such as the ones I own. I've sold properties for thousands of dollars more than what they might be appraised for by offering my special seller financing as an incentive.

As with boats, cars, and even the houses we live in, price becomes a whole lot less important if we're allowed to pay the price over a period of time. What's most important is how much my monthly payments are. This is human nature, and humans are mostly who I sell to. One other issue before I move on concerning appraisals: I do not consider appraisals beneficial to me unless the purpose is borrowing hard dollars on my property. An appraisal for the purpose of selling can be a very restrictive document to have lying around. Let's say your deal falls through and you move onto another potential buyer, but you know about the appraisal. Chances are, you'll likely need to fess up, if you're asked. I'm certain that disclosure issues would likely pop up if the appraisal shows up after you've accepted an offer for $100,000 more than it shows. Do you get the picture here?

How I Sell for Top Dollar and a Bit Extra

When I add value to properties, I not only increase the rents, but my gross rent multiplier goes up as well. My goal is a 2 point increase in the gross multiplier. For example, if I purchased the property for 6 × gross rents of $20,000 annually, or $120,000, and after two years of upgrading, rents are increased by 50 percent to $30,000, my gross rent multiplier value is now 8 × gross rents (8 × $30,000), which equals a new value of $240,000. No formal appraisal is needed because I'm selling the $30,000 annual income stream. My selling price would likely be about $240,000, should I decide to sell.

Let's say I accept an offer for full price of $240,000. I usually accept full price offers. It's my weakness. The terms I'm offering are $40,000 cash down to me, and then I'll carry the balance of $200,000 for 20 years, at 7-percent interest with amortized payments of $1,550 per month. Some may ask whether 7-percent interest is enough. Interest rates are sensitive to the times. Right now 7-percent interest is more than twice what banks are paying on certificates. I've had higher interest carrybacks in the past. But remember, rates have to do with the marketplace. Besides, there's no need to belly up to the hog line in this business. It's highly profitable without gouging your customers.

By accepting my payments over time, 240 months, I'll take in over twice the amount of my selling price ($412,000). The interest alone adds up to $172,000, or roughly $717 per month for each of those 240 months of our contract. I don't know about you, but earning $717 every month without lifting my little finger seems all right by me. Even when you deduct the cost of my pajamas every five years or so, I'm still a long way ahead.

Interest income is very powerful stuff. It will make tall buildings taller. When I was a very small boy, my dad took my sister and me on a trip to San Francisco. While we were there, he showed us the stately Wells Fargo Bank building in the heart of the city. He told us to look up. "That building is 28 stories high," he said. It wasn't a whole lot of years later that as a young man I had the occasion to look up at the Wells Fargo building again. It had grown to 58 stories. How did it grow so high, so fast? The answer, my friend, is interest income. Right then and there I decided that if interest earnings can build 58 stories this quickly for Well Fargo, it's certainly got to be good for my bank account too.

Installment Sales Stall Taxes

New investors will often disagree with my advice about not selling properties in the early years, so once again I point out that even today, after doing this stuff for more than 40 years, I'm hard pressed to think of anyone I'm aware of who made millionaire status from simply buying and selling. I have several friends who are off and on millionaires, but they always seem to hit hard times. Their lifestyle resembles something like a yo-yo. The truth is, you must keep your assets compounding to enable you to reach the big leagues. Keep your name on the deed as long as you can.

With that said, all investors must eventually consider how they wish to live during their sunset years. In case you're wondering what a "sunset investor" might look like, take a quick peek at any of my brochures or flyers with my picture on the front. That should give you a pretty fair idea. I can definitely feel the sunset creeping in under my worn-out straw hat. I'm also aware that when I leave, the real estate must stay, thus spending a good share of my equity before I depart has always been my master plan.

Installment selling is the tax term. When I sell, I take a down payment and allow the buyer to pay off the balance of my selling price over a period of time. Other than tax-deferred exchanging under Revenue Code 1031, installment sales are the next best strategy for putting off having to pay taxes. With installment sales, you're allowed to pay the tax bill as you receive the payments from your buyer. With wraparound financing, which is the way you should sell all properties with existing mortgage debt, you'll benefit even more because you'll avoid the debt reduction tax that would occur if the mortgages were assumed or taken over by your buyer. If you don't understand this, check it out with your tax person or me before you agree to a sale.

Wraparounds Provide Safety and Profits

Wraparound financing has several other major advantages besides the tax savings. First of all, you as the seller carry back a promissory note (or mortgage) and will receive just one single payment every month even if there are several unpaid mortgages on the property at the time you sell it. They're called *underlying mortgages*, and the unpaid balance of each one will be included or made part of the new wraparound mortgage you'll carry back for the buyer. That's what *wraparound* means. Whatever debt is owed on the property when you make the sale is wrapped into a single mortgage with just one payment for the total debt. When you receive your wraparound payment each month, you must first make payments to all the underlying mortgages. You keep what's left for yourself.

For example, suppose I sell my property for $400,000. At the time of sale, I'm making payments on a first mortgage of $100,000 at $800 per month. I also make $600 payments on a second mortgage, with a balance of $60,000. Obviously, my equity is $240,000 since I still owe two mortgages with an unpaid balance of $160,000. After receiving a $50,000 cash down payment, I agree to carry back a new wraparound note (or mortgage) for the balance of the sale ($350,000) with payments to me of $3,000 per month. Each month when I receive my $3,000 payment, I first pay both underlying mortgages ($800 and $600), leaving me the net amount of $1,600. The big safety feature of wraparound financing for me is that I'm dead-bang certain the underlying mortgages will be paid. I'm the one who will pay them! If my two mortgages were assumed or taken over by the new buyer, I might not know right away if he or she stops making payments as agreed, particularly if I'm receiving my payments on time, as promised. There are other ways to protect yourself, but none are any better than the control you have with wraparounds. Better to pay than be stuck!

Earning bonus profits with wraparound financing is another major advantage of wraparounds. Here we introduce the term *spread*. No, it has nothing to do with making bologna sandwiches. It has to do with the difference between the mortgage interest rates paid out and those we receive. I can substantially increase my yield with wraparound financing. For example, let's assume I designed my carryback, wraparound note on the above example. The note amount is $350,000, with payments of $3,000 per month at 8-percent interest until paid in full. Now say the interest rate of payments on the first mortgage of $100,000 is 6.5 percent, and, for the second mortgage of $60,000, payments are at a 7.0 percent rate of interest. The interest rate differences between the underlying mortgages ($100,000 at 6.5 percent and $60,000 at 7.0 percent) and the new wraparound mortgage rate of 8.0 percent is called the *spread*. Let me explain how the extra profits work. First, my profits or gain comes from selling my equity (what I own) in the property for $240,000. For that I'm being paid $50,000 cash down and $1,600 per month, including 8.0-percent interest. That's a fair deal for me, but that's all I would have received had I allowed the buyer to take over or assume the existing mortgages; however, I didn't.

Since I'll continue making payments on my first mortgage of $100,000 at an interest rate of 6.5 percent, I'll earn a 1.5-percent spread. Remember, the $100,000 mortgage is wrapped. It's part of my new $350,000 wraparound note, which earns me 8.0-percent interest. The bottom line is that I earn 8.0 percent and pay out 6.5-percent interest on money ($100,000) that doesn't even belong to me. Obviously, the same thing applies to the second mortgage ($60,000). I'll pay out 7.0-percent interest, but receive 8.0 percent on money I simply don't own or have no rights to. My earnings are a 1.0-percent spread. When you calculate the blended rate of my wraparound financing, you'll find it's higher than the 8.0-percent rate I negotiated with my buyer.

Tailoring Your Carryback Note to Your Buyer

The Number 1 reason why investors like myself are leery of selling properties for low down payments is that we don't want the property back. This can be a serious problem for sellers who retire and decide to travel around the world on the payments. What's the big danger, you ask? An example might be selling your 10-unit apartment complex to someone without any landlording experience or selling older, higher-maintenance properties to an out-of-town owner who tells you his brother-in-law will look after things. Older properties require loving care and an owner who can take care of business. When I sell and carry back the financing, I spend a good bit of effort checking out the buyer. I design my carryback note (mortgage) to fit the cash flow needs (within reason, of course) of the buyer. I want the buyers to succeed because if they don't, they'll likely default, and I'll have a mess to straighten out. You should always run a credit check on any buyer you carry financing for.

I nearly always require additional security on low-down-payment sales. Most buyers own their homes or other properties. For example, take the $400,000 sale above where I receive a $50,000 down payment. That's only 12.5 percent down, so I tell my buyer I would really like to have 25 percent down so I feel secure. Since the buyer owns a home worth $200,000 with an existing first mortgage of $100,000, I will say, "Here's what I propose we do. I'll draw up a note and deed of trust (or mortgage) in the amount of $50,000 to be a second lien or mortgage on your home. I won't charge any monthly payments if you faithfully perform on the wraparound carryback note (make all the payments as you promise), and at the end of 60 months, I'll remove (reconvey) the additional collateral note of $50,000 from your house." This arrangement protects me and doesn't cost the buyer a plugged nickel so long as he or she performs.

It certainly makes me sleep much better, and hopefully I never have to get out of my pajamas. It's called additional collateral. It's extra insurance for me, and it allows the buyer to use what he or she already owns (a home) to purchase income property with less up-front cash. It's a winner for both of us.

Appendix A

Rental and Contractor's Agreements

This appendix will give you two agreements you can use when you rent property to tenants and when you contract to have work done on properties you own. The rental agreement includes a long list that anticipates problems that may occur with some tenants so that the owner is protected. The independent contractor's agreement helps ensure that the work you want done will be done in a manner, time frame, and cost that you as owner will find acceptable, as well as to help protect you from shoddy work.

Rental Agreement

THIS AGREEMENT is made between ONE STOP HOME RENTAL COMPANY, owners or representatives for _____ _____ and

TENANTS: _____

For the rental of real property known as _____ _____.

TENANTS AGREE to pay rent for the property on a month-to-month basis starting: Date: _____. The agreed monthly rental rate shall be: $_____ per month and shall be due and payable in advance on the ___ day of every calendar month (rent due date).

TENANTS AGREE to pay last month's rent of $_____ in advance, to be used only for last month of tenancy and only after tenants give owner thirty (30) days' written notice that the property will be vacated. Tenants further agree to rent property for a minimum of six (6) months.

TENANTS AGREE to pay an advance cleaning/security deposit, which is refundable if property is left clean and undamaged and if 30-day written notice to vacate property is given. Advance cleaning/security deposit for this property is: $_____.
Owners will refund deposits within twenty-one (21) days after all keys to property have been returned. If any deposit funds are withheld, owners will provide an itemized statement showing their disposition. Tenants agree to forfeit all advance deposits if tenancy is less than six (6) months unless otherwise specified under Special Agreements, below.

TENANTS AGREE to pay a late charge of $35.00 if rent is not paid within five (5) days after rent due date. <u>Example</u>: If rent due date is on 1st of month, a late charge is due if rent is not paid by 5th day of month.

TENANTS AGREE to pay a $30.00 additional service charge on all returned checks (bounced). <u>This service charge is in addition to late charges</u> if rent payment is late because of returned check.

IT IS FURTHER UNDERSTOOD that TENANTS are responsible

for any losses to their personal property while living at this rental location. It is agreed between the parties, Owners/Tenants, that all Tenants' personal property shall be the responsibility of the Tenant only. Owners are not in any way obligated to protect or guarantee losses of Tenants' personal property.

It is agreed that only the following people or pets may live on this property: _____

GENERAL RULES AND COVENANTS

TENANTS AGREE to and shall perform according to each and all of the following general rules and covenants. Failure to abide by the rules or to perform accordingly under these rules and covenants shall be proper cause for eviction. Therefore, Tenants agree to accept and abide by the following rules and covenants.

1. TENANTS AGREE to maintain property—includes watering lawns, shrubs, and trees and to keep yards clean, meaning pick up garbage in yard and common areas. No indoor-type house furniture shall be left outside house in yard area.

2. TENANTS AGREE to use common garbage bins and containers provided by the Owners for household garbage only and shall not dispose of boxes, furniture (indoor-outdoor), tree branches, leaves, and other items not considered household.

3. TENANTS AGREE to obtain written permission from Owners or One Stop Home Rental Co. before altering the property in any manner. This applies to painting, removal of fire detection equipment (smoke alarms), building fences, cutting trees, or any changes proposed to interior of houses, apartments, or garages.

4. TENANTS AGREE to park only in assigned or designated parking spaces or driveways and to keep those areas clean. Oil or grease drippings must be kept cleaned up. Tenants further agree that no parking shall be allowed on lawns or landscaped areas. This includes Tenants' vehicles and those of all guests and/or visitors. Tenants also agree not to park in common roadways and driveways that limit access to other tenants and to emergency vehicles, such as fire trucks, ambulances, and police cars.

5. TENANTS AGREE not to repair vehicles on property if repairs take longer than one day. An exception may be allowed, with approval from the owners, for vehicle repairs that can be done inside an enclosed garage or shed and are not dangerous to the occupants of the property.

6. NONRUNNING vehicles are not allowed to remain on property for more than 7 days. Tenants agree to remove nonrunning vehicles from property and authorize the owner to remove (tow away) vehicles after 7 days from the date "Notice to Move Vehicle" is mailed to Tenant's address of record on file at One Stop Home Rental Co. This includes all vehicles parked on property, including those of Tenants, guests, or friends of Tenants and vehicles left by unknown parties.

7. TENANTS AGREE to pay the full cost of clearing and repairing all plumbing blockages, stoppages, and sewer backups caused by Tenants and their guests. These include hair in drain lines, toys found in drains or toilets, sanitary napkins flushed down toilets and general problems caused by occupants of property. This does not apply to main sewer line blockages, such as tree roots and faulty or collapsed lines in the sewer or septic systems.

8. TENANTS AGREE to perform reasonable housekeeping on a routine basis and to take appropriate steps to prevent or minimize the invasion of household pests, such as cockroaches, spiders, mice, and ants. Inside the premises Tenants further agree to routinely remove all household (kitchen) garbage from premises and provide proper cleaning and maintenance inside the house to avoid pest control problems.

9. TENANTS SHALL refrain from disturbing neighbor tenants. This rule applies to loud music, hollering, yelling, and screaming so as to adversely affect the rights and peaceful privacy of others (neighboring tenants). Police intervention and repeated violations of this rule shall be cause for eviction from the property.

10. TENANTS AGREE not to commit any acts of waste, nuisance, and destruction of property and shall agree that property will be used for residential purposes only. No commercial activity, such as sales to the public, is permitted. Tenants agree to comply with city, county, and local zoning laws governing the property.

Tenants shall agree to keep all Tenant-paid utilities turned on during tenancy. If utilities are turned off for nonpayment or if Tenants fail to have utilities turned on, then Tenants agree they are in violation of this lease agreement.

11. TENANTS AGREE that no criminal activity will be permitted on the property. This rule includes Tenants, guests, and visitors to the property. Furthermore, it shall be agreed between the parties that any violation shall be a sufficient reason for immediate eviction from the property.

12. TENANTS, UNDERSIGNED, AGREE that only those persons listed in this agreement are authorized to live on the property. No other persons may live at property without written permission from Owner. Furthermore, only those pets listed in this agreement may live at property, inside or outside the house or apartment. Tenants agree to clean up for approved pets, which includes pick-up (scooping of dog and cat doo-doo) in yards and around common areas where pets have access.

13. TENANTS AGREE to pay for all damages to the property caused by themselves, children, guests, and friends. Such repairs must be made with 7 days after said damages occur. Most common damages covered by this rule are broken windows, vehicle damage to buildings or fences and breaking or damaging property while attempting to make repairs without authorization from Owners.

Special Agreements: _____

_____

Violation of any part of the Agreement or nonpayment of rent when due shall be cause for eviction under appropriate sections of the State Code, and Tenants shall be liable for Court costs and reasonable attorneys' fees involved.

EVERY RESIDENT is jointly and separately liable for paying the full rent payment every month. EACH TENANT and CO-SIGNER hereby acknowledges that he or she has read this agreement, the general rules and covenants, understands them, and fully agrees with them without reservation. CO-SIGNERS further agree to be fully responsible for payment of rents and damages not paid by the Tenants or Residents. Signatures below constitute full acceptance and agreement, without reservation, with all terms, conditions, and rules above.

OWNER/REPRESENTATIVE   TENANT   DATE

DATE   TENANT   DATE

ONE STOP HOME RENTAL CO.
DIVISION OF JMK TRADERS   ―――――――――――――――――――――
Mailing Address: CO-SIGNER   DATE
P.O. 493039
Redding, CA 96049-3039   ―――――――――――――――――――――
                              CO-SIGNER   DATE

Independent Contractor's Agreement

TERMS AND CONDITIONS

WHEREAS <u>Jay's Rental Co.</u> (CLIENT) intends to contract with <u>"Do-Good" Apt. Service</u> (INDEPENDENT CONTRACTOR) for the performance of certain tasks; INDEPENDENT CONTRACTOR'S principal place of business is located at the following address: <u>5 Your Street</u> .

INDEPENDENT CONTRACTOR declares that he or she is engaged in an independent business and has complied with all federal, state, and local laws regarding business permits and licenses that may be required to perform the work or activities specified by this contract (see Item #1).

INDEPENDENT CONTRACTOR declares that he or she is in the business of performing the specialized work or activities specified by the terms of this agreement; further that he or she performs identical work or activities for other clients upon request. Further, independent contractor guarantees client will be satisfied with such work or activity and will provide names (3) of satisfied clients as evidence of satisfactory performance.

Name	Address	Approx Date of Work
1. Sam Slick	1000 A St.	Sep. ----
2. Joe Blow	444 Sally Ave.	Oct. ----
3. Judy Seagull	1246 Amos Dr.	Dec. ----

THEREFORE, IN CONSIDERATION OF THE FOREGOING REPRESENTATIONS AND THE FOLLOWING TERMS AND CONDITIONS, CLIENT AND INDEPENDENT CONTRACTOR AGREE THAT:

1. The INDEPENDENT CONTRACTOR shall, under his or her own control and supervision and in his or her own time—using his or her own supplies and material—complete the following jobs:

Job, Work, or Activity:	**Location:**
A. Const. 110 lineal ft. 6'0" fence	1245 East St., Rdg.
B. Paint interior 5 rooms incl. bath & kitchen	777 West Ave., Rdg.
C. Repair 2 roofs, south side, both houses	331 & 334 Meyer St., Rdg.
D. Install T1-11 siding ft. of house 36 × 10 surface	415 Grape St., Rdg.
E. _____	_____

2. All work covered by this contract agreement must be completed to the satisfaction of the CLIENT on or before <u>March 15, ----</u> (Date).

3. CLIENT may have certain supplies available in its warehouse for sale. INDEPENDENT CONTRACTOR may, at his or her sole discretion, elect to purchase from CLIENT. In the event such supplies are available, materials to be purchased and the cost thereof are as follows:

Supply Items <u>12" × 6'0" cedar</u>
<u>fencing boards</u>   Cost: <u>$1.25 per board</u>

_____   _____

_____   _____

_____   _____

4. In the event that INDEPENDENT CONTRACTOR, at his or her sole discretion, elects to rent equipment from CLIENT, the type of equipment and cost of rental are as follows:

Equipment   <u>None</u>   Cost <u>$ None</u>

_____   _____

5. INDEPENDENT CONTRACTOR shall supply all equipment, tools, materials and supplies to accomplish the designated work as specified above under Items 1 and 2.

6. INDEPENDENT CONTRACTOR shall have the right to control or direct the manner in which the jobs or activity described herein are to be performed, subject to the foregoing. CLIENT retains

the right to inspect, to stop work, to prescribe alterations, to enforce safety procedures, and generally to supervise the work to ensure its conformity with terms specified in this agreement.

7. Payments shall be made to INDEPENDENT CONTRACTOR as follows:

(a) Upon completion of the work (See Item 2) $600.00

(b) Less, cost of supplies to be purchased or equipment rented as indicated by Items 3 and 4 above $137.50

(c) Net amount payable upon completion $462.50

8. INDEPENDENT CONTRACTOR shall submit billing invoices to CLIENT, in accordance with Item 7 above.

9. This agreement shall terminate on completion of work (Item 1) and may not be terminated earlier except on 15 days' written notice.

10. Any dispute between INDEPENDENT CONTRACTOR and CLIENT concerning the terms and conditions of this agreement shall be submitted to binding arbitration pursuant to the laws of the State of ___California___.

11. All payments for work covered by this agreement are GROSS BID AMOUNTS. INDEPENDENT CONTRACTOR agrees to assume total liability for payment of all taxes including federal, state, social security and unemployment insurance. INDEPENDENT CONTRACTOR further agrees to provide his or her own worker's compensation insurance and releases CLIENT of all claims of any nature arising hereunder from this agreement.

12. The parties agree that each of the terms of this agreement is of the essence.

Executed this _3rd_ day of _March ----_, State of _California_

CLIENT:

Name: ___Jay's Rental Co.___   Name: ___"Do-Good" Apt. Service___

By: ___Jay P. DeCima, Owner___   By: ___John Doe, Owner/Operator___

Address: _12 Your St.___   Address: __5 Your St.___

City: _Redding___ State: _CA___   City: _Redding___ State: _CA___

ZIP: _00000_ Tel: _555-555-555_   ZIP: _00000_ Tel: _555-111-111_

Appendix B

Oliver Street Property Documents

This appendix gives readers three items to help them understand and manage rental properties, using the Oliver Street properties as an example. First you'll find an example of a property sketch. This is followed by a property analysis form and an example of a gross rent multiplier, created for Jay's area.

Jay's 7-Unit Property on Oliver Street

3 Houses, 2 Duplexes

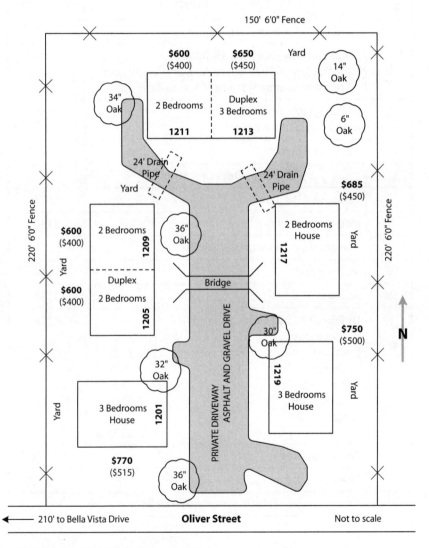

150' 6'0" Fence

$600
($400)

$650
($450)

Yard

14"
Oak

34"
Oak

2 Bedrooms | Duplex
3 Bedrooms

1211 | **1213**

6"
Oak

24' Drain
Pipe

24' Drain
Pipe

Yard

$685
($450)

220' 6'0" Fence

220' 6'0" Fence

Yard

2 Bedrooms

1209

36"
Oak

2 Bedrooms
House

1217

Yard

Yard

$600
($400)

Duplex

$600
($400)

2 Bedrooms

1205

Bridge

PRIVATE DRIVEWAY
ASPHALT AND GRAVEL DRIVE

30"
Oak

$750
($500)

N

32"
Oak

1219

3 Bedrooms
House

Yard

Yard

3 Bedrooms
House

1201

$770
($515)

36"
Oak

36"
Oak

← 210' to Bella Vista Drive **Oliver Street** Not to scale

New Rents After Fix-up: $600

Rents at Time of Purchase: ($400)

Income Property Analysis Form

Property Name: Oliver Street   **Date: Now**

Line No.	Income Data (Monthly)		Per Month
1	Total Gross Income (Present)		$3,115
2	Vacancy Allowance Min. 5% (Line 1) (Attach copy of 1040 Schedule E or provide past 12 months income statement for verification)		$156
3	Uncollectable or Credit Losses (rents due but not collected)		$156
4	Net Rental Income		$2,803
	Expense Data (Monthly)		
5	Taxes, Real Property*		$175
6	Insurance		$130
7	Management, Allowance Min. 5%		$156
8	Maintenance		$310
9	Repairs		$155
10	Utilities Paid by Owner (Monthly) Electricity $0 Water $120 Sewer $70 Gas $0 Dumpster $130 Cable TV $0 Total $320		$320
11	Total Expenses		$1,246
12	Operating Income (Line 4 – Line 11)		$1,557
	Existing Mortgage Debt		
			Monthly Payment	Due Mo/Yr
	1st Bal. Due	$62,500	$664	13 Years
	2nd Bal. Due	$31,600	$425	9 Years

(continued on the next page)

Appendix B. Oliver Street Property Documents

(new)	3rd Bal. Due	$85,900	$500	Until Paid
	4th Bal. Due	0		
	5th Bal. Due	0		
13	Totals	$180,000	(13A) $1,589	
14	Monthly Cash Flow Available (Line 12 – 13A) (Positive or Negative)			($32) Negative

Note: Line 14 shows available funds to service new mortgage debt from operation of property.

Remarks: All lines must be completed for proper analysis. Enter the actual amount on each line or enter 0.

*This $ amount should equal monthly taxes based on purchase price.

Income Property Analysis Form (continued)

Typical Gross Rent Multiplier (GRM) Chart

Jay's Area: 675 to 1100 Sq. Ft. Units—Houses and Duplexes

GRM	Description	Avg. Rent	No. Units	Monthly Income $	Annual Income $	Est. Value
11	Snob Hill	$750	7	$5,250	$63,000	$693,000
10	Premo	$740	7	$5,180	$62,160	$621,600
9	Desirable	$725	7	$5,075	$60,900	$548,100
8	Nicer	$700	7	$4,900	$58,800	$470,400
7	Average	$665	7	$4,655	$55,860	$391,020
6	Dirty	$515	7	$3,605	$43,260	$259,560
5	Filthy	$445	7	$3,115	$37,380	$186,900
4	Pigsty	$390	7	$2,730	$32,760	$131,040
3	Falling Down	$300	7	$2,100	$25,200	$75,600

This chart indicates the approximate amount (price) buyers are willing to pay for multiple
rental units in Jay's area. Although these rents and prices may be similar to those in other
locations, this chart is based on local knowledge for Jay's investment area. The estimated
value is based on condition, location, and amount of income.

Appendix C

Resources for Real Estate Investors

Newsletters

Ask for a Free Copy

Real Estate Newsletter
Robert J. Bruss
251 Park Road
Burlingame, CA 94010
800-736-1736

Trade Secrets Newsletter (Monthly)
Jay P. DeCima
KJAY Publishing
P.O. Box 491779
Redding, CA 96049
800-722-2550

CommonWealth Letters (Monthly)
Jack Miller
CommonWealth Press, Inc.
P.O. Box 21172
Tampa, FL 33622
888-282-1882

Money Maker Report (Monthly)
Jim Napier, Inc.
P.O. Box 858
Chipley, FL 32428
800-354-2072

Strategies and Solutions (6 issues annually)
John Schaub
Proserve
2677 S. Tamiami Trail, Suite 4
Sarasota, FL 34239
800-237-9222

Mr. Landlord Newsletter (monthly)
Jeffrey Taylor
Mr. Landlord, Inc.
P.O. Box 64442
Virginia Beach, VA 23467
800-950-2250

Books for Real Estate Investors

The following is a brief sampling of books that real estate investors will find useful. I recommend doing a search for other such books at Amazon.com or other online bookstores.

Brangham, Suzanne, *Housewise* (Clarkson Potter, 1987).

DeCima, Jay P., *Investing in Fixer-Uppers* (McGraw-Hill, 2003).

Kessler, A.D., *A Fortune at Your Feet* (Professonal Publishers, Inc., 2004).

Kroc, Ray, *Grinding It Out: The Making of McDonald's* (St. Martin Press, 1990).

Reed, John T., *Aggressive Tax Avoidance for Real Estate Investors*, 18th Ed. (Reed Publishing, 2004). Available at www.johntreed.com/ATA.html.

Robinson, Leigh, *Landlording: A Handy Manual for Scrupulous Landlords and Landladies Who Do It Themselves,* 9th Ed. (Express Publishing, 2003).

Schumacher, David, *Buy and Hold: 7 Steps to a Real Estate Fortune* (Schumacher Enterprises, 2004).

Real Estate Seminars and Workshops

Fixer House Camps, Fixer Jay, 800-722-2550
(learn more here:
www.reiclub.com/articles/landlording-skills-big-bucks)

Various Wealthbuilding, Jack Miller, 888-282-1882
(learn more here: cashflowconcepts.com/seminars_main.htm)

Making It Big on Little Deals, John Schaub, 800-237-9222
(learn more here: www.johnschaub.com)

Acquisition Techniques, Pete Fortunato, 727-397-1906
(learn more here:
www.peterfortunato.com/pages/692250/index.htm)

Various, Jeffrey Taylor, 800-950-2250
(learn more here about Jeffrey Taylor and other seminars:
www.realestatecoursereviews.com)

Listings

Real Estate Investor Clubs and Associations Nationwide

Creative Real Estate Magazine, A.D. Kessler, 858-756-1441.

Index

Index

Index

Index

About the Author

"Fixer Jay" DeCima is a seasoned real estate investor-landlord with over 45 years of experience and 200 rental houses to show for his efforts. Jay is also a successful career changer having worked more than 20 years for the telephone company.

Twenty years ago, Jay began teaching others his high-profit fix-up techniques and landlording skills. Today he is widely regarded as king of the fixer-uppers on the national teaching circuit.

Jay conducts his popular hands-on house-fixing workshops in his hometown of Redding, California, four times annually, where students visit Jay's properties and learn the ropes first-hand.

Trade Secrets, Jay's monthly newsletter, is the only newsletter written specifically for hands-on, do-it-yourself investors and career changers. Write for a free copy to: Fixer Jay, KJAY Co., Box 491779B, Redding, CA 96049-1779. Print "T.S. copy" on the envelope.

To see Jay's bimonthly investor tip, visit www.fixerjay.com.